J. Dickinson Hunt

The Union restored by legal Authority

Its past Errors, its present Restoration, and its bright Future

J. Dickinson Hunt

The Union restored by legal Authority
Its past Errors, its present Restoration, and its bright Future

ISBN/EAN: 9783337153588

Printed in Europe, USA, Canada, Australia, Japan

Cover: Foto ©ninafisch / pixelio.de

More available books at **www.hansebooks.com**

THE

UNION RESTORED

BY LEGAL AUTHORITY:

ITS PAST ERRORS, ITS PRESENT RESTORATION, AND
ITS BRIGHT FUTURE.

By J. DICKINSON HUNT, M. D.

CONTAINING ILLUSTRATIONS OF

PUBLIC AND PRIVATE RIGHTS, AND PUBLIC AND PRIVATE WRONGS.

NEW YORK:
PRINTED AT No. 20 NORTH WILLIAM STREET.
1865

CONTENTS.

CONTENTS.

PREFACE.

THE reasoning and illustrations contained in the following pages are intended to direct the intelligent American citizen in some of those trains of thought which he ought to prosecute while looking forward to the enjoyment of that *Deed* of *Trust*—that invaluable Triune Estate—*Life*, *Liberty* and *Property*, received and conveyed in *Trust* to us for our use by that long list of Patriots and Sages, who at the hazard of all that was dear to man, signed the Declaration of Independence, as also those who framed the great charter of our liberties. Long live their memory, and cherished be their names in every American bosom; and while true merit is esteemed and appreciated or virtue honored, mankind will never cease to revere and ever to remember, with hearts full of unfeigned gratitude, those venerable Fathers for these inestimable immunities which were bought with a price, not of silver or of gold, nor of precious stones, but with the sacrifice of many pure and precious lives, and with the sanguinary flow of life's vital fluid, which was freely spilled upon the plains of this now happy country.

The Author was induced to engage in the discussion of the subject of regeneration and reconstruction of the Union, from a consideration that many vague and erroneous conceptions are entertained among the free-born American people in regard to the nature of the unity of the Federal Government and its retinue of States. In elucidating the train of thought here produced, he has brought forward without hesitation the discoveries of modern science and applied its principles to this Republic, established upon Democratic principles, in harmony with the scale by which all things ascend to UNITY. The writer uses the word principles according to the common acceptation of the term; but to speak more philosophically it is that one great principle which binds all things together.

He has carefully avoided every thing that might appear like vague or extravagant conjecture ; and he trusts that the opinions he has broached and the conclusions he has deduced, will generally be found to accord with the analogies of Nature and the dictates of Revelation. He is aware that he has many prejudices to encounter, arising from the vague and indifferent manner in which the subject of Life, Liberty, and Property have been hitherto treated, and the want of those expansive views of the one great principle which binds them together, and which every American citizen should endeavor to obtain ; but he feels confident that those who are best qualified to appreciate his sentiments, will treat with candor an attempt to elucidate a subject that may serve as a mirror for all the sons of Columbia to behold themselves, and try the Representatives of this gigantic young Republic by testing the capacity of mind for the concentration of this thundering plurality—this motive power of Democratic rule.

The duality of motion renders it necessary that the author publish this work in the dual divisions of the individual man and Government, in order that it may correspond with this dual Democratic Republic, and with the dual divisions of public and private rights—public and private wrongs. With proper inculcations of the precepts and practice of our fathers, and particularly to place in a proper light before the uninitiated, the reflection of a Republic established upon Democratic principles, with the indelible mark of truth and nature stamped upon it.

There is a centre in every circle, and a central idea in every system in Heaven and on Earth. The Declaration of Independence, Confederation and Constitution, forms the centre of the Federal Government, around which the States revolve—a centre of the municipal government of States around which counties revolve, and a centre of the sub-municipalities or counties which, like the Federal Government, have a retinue of towns for their attendants, being irradiated by their beams and revolving around their attractive influence. Upon this unity, this centre, the author has erected his superstructure, which he is vain enough to imagine may, with perhaps some variations, withstand the storms and tempests of time. Seizing upon the unity of all things with a true analytical grasp, *combining, comparing* and *discriminating, by applying them to the practical end in view,* he has been enabled to fill up the chasms with something of his own, thereby correcting as he humbly hopes some errors. Instead of traversing the system of American Law in a circle, he has traversed it in a line agreeable to the principles of engineering and the views of Lord Bacon, who once remarked, that "The reason medical knowledge had not advanced, was because physicians reasoned too much in a circle and not enough in a line." The author attributes the present contradictory and conflicting opinions on legal science to the same cause, and has made the guage points of a line on the engineer's rule his guiding star, bringing forth arguments which he is not aware have been taken notice of by authors, when treating on the subject of legal science. He has endeavored to illustrate these in minute detail, and in a popular manner, so as to be within the comprehension of every reader, and perhaps more convincing than the subtle and refined disquisitions of metaphysicians. He trusts, that the force of the whole combined, will be found to amount to as high a degree of moral demonstration as can be expected in relation to a subject which Blackstone informs us can only be conceived by human reason. His method of arriving at facts may appear crude and undigested to many minds, but his object has been to get at facts in that way and manner by which he could make himself best understood, whether by *comparison*, *anecdote* or *fable*. And, therefore, he is in hopes that the *matter* and not the *manner*, will be the guiding star to the reader. Facts, when disjointed, are the mere bricks or material with which the builder of all systems must work. And to deny to any man the merit of being the architect of a great edifice of truth on that account, would be just as reasonable as to ascribe the merit of St. Paul's Cathedral to the donkeys and other beasts of burden Sir Christopher Wren necessarily employed in carrying the marble and mortar composing it.

The practical reflections and remarks embodied in this work will not, the author is persuaded, be considered by any of his readers as either unnecessary or inappropriate to the subject of regeneration and reconstruction, under the newly developed power of the Constitution over the people to prevent individual rights from interfering with the safety of the States. In doing this, it has not been the design of the writer to contribute to the political elevation of any man ; he has aimed rather to display the spirit and principles of the American nation, and to exhibit by the death of an individual, the nature of the relation which that nation sustains to its public men. He has endeavored, in this way, to throw some light upon the character of our institutions, and to illustrate in some degree, the spirit of the nation and the age.

The philosophy of history is more valuable than facts. Remarkable as are the incidents both in the life and death of Abraham Lincoln, they would not have attracted the particular attention of the writer, if he had not believed, that in laying them before the public, an opportunity would be furnished of discussing political principles which are of vital importance to the prosperity of our country. They rouse the sluggish to exertion, give increased energy to the most active intellect, excite a salutary vigilance over our public functionaries, and prevent that apathy which has proved the ruin of Republics. Like the electric spark, they dispel from the political atmosphere the latent causes of disease and death. With these few remarks, he consigns his work, with the hope that it may not be altogether unworthy of attention. That it may tend to impress all freemen to duly consider the price of the privileges they enjoy, and not resign them into the hands of others, to consider liberty the greatest political blessing that God can bestow on his creature man, to expand the believer's conception of the attributes of the Divinity, and the glory of that inheritance which is reserved in heaven for the faithful, and to excite, in the mind of every reader, an urgent desire to cultivate those dispositions and virtues which will prepare him for the enjoyment of celestial bliss, is the author's most sincere wish, as it was the great object he had in view when engaged in its composition and compilation.

REMARKS.

By the motion of man's hands the pyramids were produced. The same motion, acting *reversely* might make them vanish from the plains where they have stood the wonders of centuries. If the identical powers, which may render a temple a heap of ruins, be applied in the opposite way for its preservation and defence, why may not the *motive* power of a physical agent, which, wrongly administered, has destroyed the life of a nation, be employed, in a right direction, to preserve its existence.

"Philosophy, wisdom, and liberty, support each other : he who *will not* reason is a bigot, he who *cannot* is a fool, and he who *dares* not is a slave !"—(Sir William Drummond.) The *motive* power of a Republic must be greater and more rapid than that of a despotism, inasmuch as all such movements can only result from the action of mind on matter. What great things, therefore, does the Lord God require of those who are in great places representing this gigantic Republic in which is concentrated the thundering plurality—the motive power of Democratic rule, MIND, is an emanation from the Deity, it goes forth in its spiritual dignity, connected with, yet distinct from, the grosser elements of life. In the contemplation of this great attribute, we stand on the farthest banks of reason's Rubicon. We are aware of its existence by its manifestations, but its origin rests in the Arcana of the works and wonders of God.

Of the essence of this element I frankly acknowledge my ignorance, and desire to avoid entering on a fruitless analysis of that mysterious principle which shed its intelligent light on the dwellers in Eden, has accompanied succeeding generations of humanity, and will outlive in a purer condition in another and better state of being the last tottering vital frame that lingers on the verge of a material world. It is, however, in some way connected with matter, and the medium of that connection is electricity.

Electricity must, therefore, be considered the great *vivifying principle* of nature by which she carries on most of her operations. It is the most subtle and active of all fluids. "It is a kind of soul which pervades and quickens every part of nature." It is, physiologically considered, the connection between mind and matter ; the power, but not the essence of vitality. It is, politically considered, the connector between the mind of the people and the matter of government ; the power, but not the essence of political life. It is not the laws of the State, nor the laws of the United States, nor the people or matter composing the States ; but it is the arrangement of that matter, and the eternal principle of law concentrated in the mind of the people, and applied to that arrangement, that sets the political machinery of the government in harmonious motion. This eternal principle or power is different throughout the vast creation, moving and acting in all bodies, and giving them certain properties peculiar to their own organization and the situation in which they are found. This principle, then, my friends, is nothing less than the great I AM, the builder of the universe and the upholder of all its parts, acting according to certain laws which he himself has fixed, and which are immutable.

CHAPTER I.

MAN LAST CREATED TO RULE OVER ALL — AMERICA THE LATEST FOUND OF THE CONTINENTS OF OUR EARTH, TO GIVE THE FIRST EXAMPLE OF THAT TRULY POPULAR SYSTEM OF GOVERNMENT, THAT SYSTEM SOON TO CONTROL ALL NATIONS — THE TRUTH OF THE DUALITY OF MOTION IS MIGHTY AND MUST PREVAIL.

MAN, in the plenitude of his mental powers, the master spirit of a material world, is a subject which must, at all times, engage the attention of the moralist, as he looks, from the smallest atom scattered in his path, to the boundless intelligence of a great first cause.

The gradual additions to the systems of animal existence, from the zoöphyte, scarcely to be distinguished from a vegetable, deprived of the organs of locomotion, chained to the rock which is at once its cradle and its grave, to man, with his majestic intellect and perfect cerebral organization, is a subject which cannot be contemplated without giving rise to admiration at the progressive advancement in the chain of animated nature, and gratitude for the superiority of those gifts which stand as the crown of eternity on the capital of the living column, decorating the brow of the master spirit who directs and controls the whole.

Therefore, let me beg of you to look upon me only as a living column, on the capital of which stands the lamp of reason, reflecting the light of revelation on all surrounding intelligencies that come within the purifier of its brilliant rays, and serve as a beacon to draw you into the channel of contemplation and moor you safely into the exercise of those noblest gifts of heaven—the reasoning faculties given you by the great Architect of the Universe.

On the higher powers of Observation, Comparison, Comprehension and Direction, termed *Mind* or *Intellect*, man stands pre-eminent above all animals ; in so far as regards the more immediate observation of certain things around him, he is nevertheless excelled in some respects by many. The eagle has a finer and farther sight ; the hearing of the mole is more acute ; the dog and the vulture distinguish odors wholly inappreciable by him ; not a few of the wilder denizens of the forest have even a keener sense of taste and touch. In mere preceptive power, then, the beasts of the field are, in some things, permitted to surpass us ; while the sagacity of the elephant and the dog, the courage and emulation of the horse, the foresight of the ant, the cunning of the fox, and the social and building habits of the beaver, declare to us—however unpleasing the announcement—that others of God's creatures besides ourselves possess the elements, at least, of that reason upon which we so highly pride ourselves. To the greater degree of complexity—perhaps I should rather say *completeness* of his cerebral organization—to his more perfect development of that source of all reasoning power, the brain, man assuredly owes this corresponding increase in the number and force of his reasoning faculties. The more complete mechanism of his prehensible organ the hand, gives him the power to execute what his head conceives, in a degree of perfectibility that we look for in vain in the works of any other tribe of the animal kingdom. Look at "man's full, fair front ;" it is a superadded, not a superfluous part ; the more it diminishes and recedes, the nearer you will find its possessor to be akin to the brute.

But, my friends, the rudiments of every portion of this instrument of man's reasoning faculties, this directing brain, variously developed, may be detected in almost every link of the great chain of animated beings of which he is confessedly the chief. To every variety of race that animates the globe, whether in external or internal configuration, we have undeniably many features of relationship ; nor let us spurn even the meanest and most shapeless as beneath our notice ; for of every organic production of their common maker, man, while yet in the womb of his parent, has been the type ! his foetal form successively partaking of the nature of the worm, fish and reptile, and rapidly traversing still higher gradations in the scale of organized existence, to burst at last upon the view in all the fullness and fairness of the perfect infant. But it is not in his outward form only that he passes through these various gradations of animal life. From Comparative Anatomy we also learn that each of his separate internal organs, on first coming into foetal existence, assumes the lowest type of the same organ in the animal kingdom ; and it is only by successive periodic transformations that it gradually approaches to the degree of completeness in which we find it in the new-born child. The heart of the embryo infant is a mere canal, nearly straight at first, and then slightly curved, corresponding exactly with the simplicity of heart of insect life—that of the snail, and other insects of the lowest *crustacea* tribe, for

example. And not the heart alone, but each and all of the several
organs and systems of the body are brought to their perfection by
periodic additions and superadditions of the simpler and more
complex parts of the same organs and systems of the several
orders of animals, from the least noble to the highest class of all,
the mammalia, of which man is the head. Man, proud man! then
commences his fœtal life in reality, a worm! and even when he has
come into the world, and has breathed and cried, it is long before
the child possesses the mental intelligence of many of the adult
brutes. In this respect man is, for a period, lower than the monkey,
the monkey he so hates and despises for its caricature likeness of
himself. Between the same man in his maturity and his animal
fellow-creatures, we perceive many differences; the resemblances,
being infinitely more numerous, escape our memory.

Are not the higher order of animals, and most of the very
lowest, propagated by sexes? Does not the female endure her
period of travail like woman, and produce and suckle her young in
a similar manner? Have not animals senses to see, hear, smell, taste
and touch, and has·not each its respective language of sounds and
signs by which it conveys its meaning to the other individuals of its
race? Nay, have not animals many of man's passions and emo-
tions, most of his sympathies and antipathies, his power of choice
and resistance, the knowledge, by *comparison*, who is their friend
and who their foe—*reflection*, whom to conciliate, whom to attack;
where to hide, and when to show themselves; the *memory* of injury
and kindness; *imitation*, and consequent docility—in some instances,
simulation and dissimulation, each pursuing its own mode of artifice?
Do not their young, too, as in the instance of the child, gambol and
play, and like it leave off both as they grow older for other plea-
sures? And yet there are persons of a temper so unphilosophical
as to deny them mind! Does man possess a greater mental superiority to the dog, or as great as the dog has over the oyster? Of
mental, as of physcial power, there are gradations. If we have stupid and clever men, so have we stupid and clever animals, according to their respective races. But there are dogs that will observe,
calculate and act more rationally than some human fools you may
see every day. When did you find the dog prostrating himself
before a figure of his own making, asking it questions, supplicating
it, and howling, and tearing his hair, because it answered him not?
Which of all the brutes quarrels with his fellow brute for going
his own road, whether circuitous or otherwise, to a town or village,
that does not concern the other in the least? Or which of all the
animal tribes manifest such a paucity of intellect as, more than once,
to mistake the same false signs for real sense, imposture for integrity,
gravity for wisdom, antiquity for reality? Never, in my life, my
friends, did I see the dog or monkey implicitly submitting himself
to another of his race in matters that especially interested himself.
The monkey, for example, instead of trusting to the authority of
his fellow-monkey, in a spirit of laudable curiosity, always handles

with his tiny fingers, and *examines* with his quick, prying eyes, every thing that takes his fancy; in no single instance that I remember did I ever see him allow himself to be taken by the ears. Even in his language of chatter and gibber he never seems to mistake the meaning of his comrades, never takes one *sign* in two or more *senses*—senses the most opposite—so as to get confused and bewildered in his manner or his actions. Can you always say this of man? Have you never heard him, even in his discussion on this very subject, one moment charging every thing of animal intellect to *Mind*, at another to *Instinct*—instinct which, to have a meaning at all, must mean this—right action *without* experience—such as the infant taking its mother's breast as soon as born, or the chick picking up grain the moment it leaves the shell. True, the chick may mistake a particle of chalk for a grain of wheat, even as the infant may mistake his nurse's finger for the nipple of his mother. Experience corrects the error of both; and this correction of error is one of the first efforts of the three mental faculties, *Observation*, *Comparison* and *Reflection*. It is with these identical faculties that both men and animals perceive a relationship between two or more things, and act in regard to such things according to their respective interests—rightly in some instances, wrongly in others. The correction of to-day of the errors of yesterday is the chief business of man. As he grows in years, his experience of things enlarges, and his judgment as to their true value and relationship to himself becomes more and more matured. The brutes, then, have the very same intellectual faculties variously developed, which when stimulated to their utmost in MAN, and with the assistance of higher *moral* faculties become GENIUS—if by genius is meant the discovery of relationship in nature hitherto undiscovered, and leading, as all such discoveries do, to practical results beyond cotemporary anticipation—Newton's system and Watt's steam-engine for example.

My friends, you now clearly see, that in the power of gaining knowledge by experience—call it *Mind*, Reason, Intellect, or what you please—the beast of the field partakes in common with man, though not in the same degree; yet both partake of it in a degree equal to the particular condition of exigencies in which they are individually or socially placed. For animals, like men, have their cities and sentinels—their watchwords of battle, siege and defence. Man, less gifted in either of these respects, first fashioned his sword and shield, and his armour of proof. It was only after the experience of centuries he reached, by higher mental efforts, to the knowledge necessary for the construction of the musket, the cannon and the other munitions of modern warfare. Necessity was the mother of his invention here, as indeed in every other instance; but by this also the lower animals profit. What but necessity enables our domestic animals to change their habits so as to live in peace, harmony or slavery with man? even as necessity obliges man enslaved to do and bear for his fellow men things the most repugnant to his nature How different the habits of the domestic dog from the dog or wolf of the prairie, from which he originally sprang ! In the wilderness, the one would all but perish for want, till stern necessity should *teach* him to hunt down his prey; the other would require stripes and blows through successive generations before he could be *taught*, like the shepherd's dog, to come at his name, and to drive the sheep at his master's call, or *arithmetically* to single out from the herd two, three or more, and watch or urge them on at his bidding. To deny animal's mind is to deny them design, without which, putting mere *instinct* apart, neither men nor animals act in any manner or matter. The great DESIGNER of the UNIVERSE, in the creation of the first crystal, showed this. He proclaimed it when he made the sexes of the vegetable kingdom; when, by the zoophyte or plant-animal, he united the vegetable to the lowest link of the animal world he made his design still more manifest. When he further progressively developed his plan of insect, fish and reptile life, and added the higher animals last of all, before he completed the chain with Man, their master, he showed not only design, but unity of design; and when to men and animals he gave a power neither the crystal nor the vegetable possesses—the power of following out designs of their own making—he imbued them both with a portion of His Spirit, varying in degree; but to each he gave it in a measure equal to their respective wants and necessities. Deny this, and you deny God—you deny God's works and words; words upon which the question of *interpolation* can never arise: for every leaf of every plant is a letter of His alphabet; every tree a combination of the letters composing it; and every hill, valley and stream—every tribe of men and animals, so many sentences by which we may perceive His will and deduce His law. The stars and constellations of stars, and their periodic motions, teach, even to our frail senses, the analogies which subsist in this respect between the motions of man's body and all the movements of Nature. In their harmony of design, they give us an insight into the UNITY of the ETERNAL. And we find embodied in them a principle by which we not only may know the past and present, but to a certain extent read the future, in its dim outline of twilight and shadow. In all humility, then, let us *inwardly* prostrate ourselves before the Omnipotent: but let us at the same time beware of that *outward* mock humility which too often leads to religious pride, and engenders any thing but Christian charity ; and let it rather be our delight to trace resemblances and harmonies than to see in Nature only discords and differences. The world, the Universe, is a UNITY; and in no single instance do we find a perfect independence in any one thing pertaining to it. Betwixt man and the lower animals, we have traced, link by link, the chain of contiguity—mental as well as corporeal.

Like them he comes into the world, and like them his body periodically grows, decays, and dies. *From* the earth and *to* the earth, the matter composing our bodies comes and goes many times even in the brief space of our mortal existence. In this the human system resembles a great nation, the inhabitants of which, in the course of years, are constantly changing, while the same nation, like the body, betrays no other outward appearance of change than what naturally belongs to the periods of its rise, progress, maturity or tendency to decay. In this mirror, though imperfectly drawn, you may behold the harmony, connection, unity of all things.

We now pass to the consideration of those alterations of the American Government, termed the United States, and periodic movements of the people.

With Luther's insurrectionary upheaval in the religious world, commenced the mental and moral preparation of mankind for the acceptance of popular institutions and right of self-government, the Democratic Principle of which Cromwell was the first forcible expression, and Napoleon Bonaparte, in his earlier triumphs over kings and empires, the armed and irresistible assertion. False to the ideas which caused his elevation, this Napoleon was hurled from the throne he sought to build on the ruins and with the materials of prostrate popular liberty; and it was thus reserved by an Allwise Providence for this latest found continent of our earth, to give the first example of that truly popular system of government—soon to be the controlling idea of all nationalities—which had the moral sublimity and practical virtues of George Washington, who was educated in the University of Nature, to hold the reins and guide it through its experimental stage. Byron exclaims at the close of his Ode to Napoleon: ". Where shall the eye rest, weary of gazing on the great; where find a glory that is not criminal, a pomp that is not contemptible? Yes, there is a man, the first, the last, the best of all—the Cincinnatus of the West, whom envy itself does not hate. The name of Washington has been bequeathed to us to make humanity blush that such a man is alone in history." Is Washington as great as Byron makes him? Yes, as we shall soon see, if we compare him with the most illustrious personages. Take, for example, that Cæsar, who has dazzled men to such a degree that each vies with the other in pardoning his crimes and bowing before the greatness of his misdeeds. Washington does not pale before this hero of the Roman Empire. Doubtless the American General had neither the mind nor the resources of the Conqueror of Pharsalia; he lived in a poor and frugal community, and his fellow-citizens resembled the contemporaries of Cincinnatus more than those of Cicero; but what a moral difference there is between these two men, and considering, only Political Genius, how great is the one and how small the other. If in these two rivals we consider what belongs to the man and what belongs to the nature of the age, I mean the will, Washington does not yield to Cæsar. Once entered upon their career, neither ever quitted or drew back. Cæsar, to impose his will on the world and to expel therefrom the very name of Liberty; nothing restrained him; he slew a million of men to attain his end. Washington sought to defend and consolidate the Liberty of his country, and nothing arrested him either; he braved the halter and ignominy to free his menaced country; he rejected with contempt the crown which his army offered him, and which he might have accepted without being taxed with ambition. A dictator, he had no other care than Liberty, no other love than the Republic. Cæsar and Washington both succeeded; both founded an empire, and bequeathed to the future their example and their idea: their work will judge them. The despotism that Cæsar established gave the omnipotence to one master, and condemned a whole people to live by the will of a single man. This reign of a day, by founding the Empire, cost the world centuries of irresistible decline. The imperial administration, one of the best planned systems ever invented, wore out Roman society to such a degree that even Christianity did not revive it; new races were needed to regenerate the exhausted blood. Washington established a wise and well ordered Republic; he left to the future, not the fatal example of triumphant crime, but the beneficent example of Patriotism and Virtue. In less than fifty years, thanks to the powerful impetus to Liberty, we have witnessed the rise of an empire, founded not on conquest, but on peace and industry; an empire which, before the end of the century, will be the greatest in the civilized world, and which, if it remain faithful to the idea of its founders, if ambition does not arrest the tide of its fortune, will offer to the world the unheard of spectacle of a Republic of a hundred millions of men, richer, happier and more brilliant than the monarchies of the Old World. This is the work of Washington! Despite all the lustre of his genius, Cæsar has left a sinister name, which is the symbol of despotism. The name of Washington is greater than the founder of an Empire; Washington opens a new era in history. Greater than Cæsar; he has undone the work of the Roman; he has put an end to the fatal divorce Cæsar introduced upon the earth; he has resuscitated Liberty. And while true merit is esteemed and virtue honored, mankind will never cease to revere the memory of this great hero; and, while gratitude has a seat in the human breast, the praises of Washington will dwell on every American tongue. But why do I attempt to eulogize the name of Washington when bards and poets have long since hung their harps on the willow in despair of expressing his just merits. I, of course, can add nothing; as well might I light a taper to assist the effulgent rays of heaven's bright luminary at noon-day to light the earth. But he is gone, and his loss clothes a nation in heartfelt mourning, and we can now only say in the language of the poet,

> "The car of victory, the plume, the wreath,
> Defend not from the bolt of fate the brave;
> No note the clarion of renown can breathe
> To charm the long night of the lonely grave,
> Nor check the headlong haste of time's o'erwhelming wave."

Enough has been said to demonstrate that the happiness and perpetuation of nations and governments do not consist in an external show of pomp and grandeur, nor the apparent strength of their walls, but very much depends upon the genial diffusion of light and knowledge in the minds of the people, and upon their honesty, integrity, virtue and patriotism. No one, in the least acquainted with history, will deny that insatiable ambition almost invariably leads its victim to ruin. The first *Napoleon* was not satisfied when the diadem of France was placed upon his brow. He was controlled by an inordinate ambition, and pandering to that element of his nature, he sought to bring all Europe within his aspiring grasp, and St. Helena furnishes the sequel. The nature of Jeff. Davis, in this respect, is not unlike that which displayed itself so conspicuously in Napoleon. Davis attained a proud place among his countrymen, and was honored with positions that placed him almost on the topmost pinnacle of authority. But, like Napoleon, his ambition was unsatisfied, his craving for power and eminence was unappeased. He aspired to the position of chief ruler of half, perchance of all, the United States, and, with that object before him, he hesitated at nothing, scrupled at nothing. He willfully branded the mark of treason upon his heart, he defiled the flag of the Union which he had gallantly fought under in Mexico, he sought to destroy the Government that had raised him from obscurity to high position, and connived at the greatest outrage against his country and her defenders. His insatiable thirst for power induced him to plunge his native land into the horrors of civil war. His overreaching aspirations filled his brain with the hopes of building up an empire, of which he should be the recognized head, and he scrupled not to make his country a modern Golgotha, if only the great object of his ambition could be obtained by it. The "Confederacy" which he attempted to erect at first gave promise that Jeff.'s dream of a slave empire would be realized. It expanded until nearly half the States of the Union embraced the dogma of secession. Then came the reaction, and the limits of Jeff.'s fabric began to contract. Gradually the vision of power faded, the area of the "Confederacy" dwindled away before the spirit of Northern patriotism, and Jeff. was awakened from his dream of ambition to find that he is circumscribed by bars and bolts to a dominion only ten by fifteen feet in extent, and bounded by the four substantial walls of a prison cell. A confederacy compressed into such proportions is enough to make the light of Jeff.'s ambition burn low in the socket; but the prospect that it will be still further contracted to six feet by two, and bounded by his mother earth, is enough to extinguish the most inordinate ambition of this bold and reckless man, of whom the assassin of Abraham Lincoln was but the impersonation. Deny it who will, this dastardly act came from the aristocratic circle of the South. Some profess to deplore the crime, but Jefferson Davis, upon hearing it, took the language of another murderer: "If it were done, then 'twere better it should be well done."

Since the days of Washington the nation has given birth to many men of worth and excellence, but none resembled him in head, in heart and purpose, more than Abraham Lincoln, who, in the full fruition of his glorious work, has been struck from the roll of living men by the pistol-shot of an assassin who had been educated up to this height of crime by the teachings of our "copperhead" oracles, and by the ambition of fulfilling those instructions which he received from Richmond. Perhaps never in history has Providence been more conspicuous than in that recent procession of events where the final triumph was wrapped in the gloom of tragedy. It will be our duty to catch the moral of this stupendous drama.

For the second time in our history, the country has been summoned by the President to unite, on an appointed day, in commemorating the character and services of the dead. The first, as I have already told you, was on the death of Washington, when, as now, a day was set apart for simultaneous eulogy throughout the land, and cities, towns and villages all vied in tribute. More than half a century has passed since this early service to the memory of the Father of his Country, and now it is repeated in memory of Abraham Lincoln. Thus are Washington and Lincoln associated in the grandeur of their obsequies. But this association is not accidental. It is from the nature of the case, and because the part which Lincoln was called to perform resembled in character the part which was performed by Washington. The work left undone by Washington was continued by Lincoln. Kindred in service, kindred in patriotism, each was naturally surrounded at death by kindred homage. One sleeps in the east, and the other sleeps in the west; and thus, in death as in life, one is the embodiment of the other. The two might be compared after the manner of Plutarch; but it will be enough for the present if we glance only at certain points of resemblance and of contrast, so as to recall the part which each performed. Each was at the head of the Republic during a period of surprising trial; and each thought only of the public good, simply, purely, constantly, so that single hearted devotions to country will always find a synonym in their names. Each was the national chief during a time of successful war. Each was the representative of his country at a great epoch of history. But here, perhaps, the resemblance ends and the contrast begins. Unlike in origin, conversation and character, they were unlike also in their *ideas*, except so far as each was the servant of his country. The war conducted by Washington was unlike the war conducted by Lincoln, as the peace which crowned the arms of the one was unlike the peace which began to smile upon the other. The two wars did not differ in the scale of operations, and in the stamp of mustered hosts, more than in the ideas involved. The first was for National Independence; the second was to make the Republic one and indivisible, on the indestructible foundations of Liberty and Equality. The first only cut the connection with the mother country, and opened the way to the duties and advantages of popular government. *The second will have failed unless it performs*

2

all the original promises of that declaration which our fathers took upon their lips when they became a nation. In the relation of cause and effect the first was the natural precursor and herald of the second. National Independence was the first epoch in our history, and such was its importance that Lafayette boasted to the First Consul of France, that, though its battles were but skirmishes, they decided the fate of the world.

Fellow-citizens, in the life and character of Abraham Lincoln you have discerned his simple beginnings, have watched his early struggles, have gratefully followed his consecration to those truths which our fathers declared, have hailed him as the twice-elected head of the Republic, have recognized him at a period of national trial as the representative of the *unfulfilled promises* of our fathers, even as Washington was the representative of National Independence; and you have beheld him struck down, at the moment of victory, when rebel resistance was everywhere succumbing. Reverently we acknowledge the finger of the Almighty, and pray that all our trials may not prove futile, but that the promises of the fathers may be fulfilled, so that all men shall be equal before the law, and government shall stand only on the consent of the governed—two self-evident truths which the Declaration of Independence has announced. Washington met the power of the British lion, and gave liberty and equal rights to the people of America. Lincoln met the power of private wrongs, and restored public rights to their original purity. Thus, in truth, may it be said that Washington was the Father, and Abraham Lincoln the Saviour, of his country. In this mirror, though imperfectly drawn, you can plainly see that state sovereignty has been annihilated, and Abraham Lincoln consolidated a more perfect *Union*, and all the nations of the world will acknowledge us a nation cemented and sealed by his blood. He has destroyed that great political heresy of State Rights. He has made a complete Union, which never existed before. We had a Union, but he has raised it more firmly on its centre under the blessed provisions of the Constitution. He has developed the war-power of this Constitution—its power over the national finances—the power of the people to prevent individual aspirations from interfering with the safety of the State. He has established the right of the Government to the services of every citizen in sustaining the nation. These principles, so firmly established, will live in history as fundamental truths to protect this nation against internal assault and external enemies. He has accomplished the regeneration of this country; regenerated its nationality in freedom. Death was necessary to resurrection and immortality. The seed must die before it can be quickened into fruitfulness; God's hand lifted up our nation to make it a power among nations. Its representative died that the cause of freedom might live; and it shall live until the coming of Him whose right it is to reign shall abolish all human governments. In a pure and high-toned Christian spirit, directed by the hand of God, our lamented Chief Magistrate drew the line of demarkation between public and private rights, which severed for ever (as I hope in God) special privileges from the hand of power. Believing, as he did, that the Constitution had established a government, with the highest attribute of sovereignty, and that to subvert its authority was rebellion, and to "levy war against it was treason," and being guided by the events, as God had showed them to him, he has proved to the world that there is no power extrinsic to that of the National Government by which its powers can be rightly resisted or its obligations impaired, and that the authority of the United States within its sphere is supreme. This is a *vital principle.* It was so regarded by the framers of the Constitution, and they have secured it in the most explicit and emphatic terms : "This Constitution, and the laws made pursuant thereunto, SHALL BE THE SUPREME LAW OF THE LAND; *and the judges in every State shall be bound thereby, any thing in the Constitution or laws of any State to the contrary notwithstanding.*" And, to render this effective, they provided that the Government which they had created should be the final judge of the extent of its own powers and the meaning of its laws. To this end they established a judicial department, as a co-ordinate branch of the Government, to expound and enforce the provisions of the Constitution and acts of Congress. Nor is this all. In order that the laws of the United States should be practically, as well as theoretically supreme, they created an Executive Department, clothed with full power to enforce the laws. And thus a Government, paramount in all its departments, was established. Therefore, fellow-countrymen, be assured that the Constitution and the laws made under it cannot be overridden by State laws. The laws of the United States bear the same relation to a State as the laws of a State do to an individual. Remember this, and do not forget it in the practical application.

The disaffected, at different times, in various sections of the Union, have earnestly sought for some legal mode of resisting legislative authority ; but it has been in vain. There is no such anomalous middle ground between submission and rebellion ; and this last extreme has, at last, been reached ; *secession is but another name for rebellion.* It is vain to contend for a constitutional right to overthrow the Constitution, and legal right to destroy all law. This may serve as a glass for all true sons of Columbia to behold, not only the absurdity of these distinctions, but also the utter nothingness and vanity of the many disputes that daily occur in politics, whether municipal and federal acts, resembling each other, and amenable to the same eternal principle of law, should be called by one name or another. In the language of Hobbs : "Words are wise men's counters, they do but reckon by them ; but they are the money of fools, that value them by the authority of an Aristotle, a Cicero, a Thomas Aquinas, or any other doctor."

It is often said that the Constitution does not contemplate making war upon a State. If by this is meant only that a State, as a political body, is not to be compelled to execute the laws of the United States, it is true; because these laws act directly upon individuals, and are not to be enforced by State authority, but by National instrumentalities. In other words, we have a Government and not a mere confederacy.

But if by the proposition that the Constitution does not contemplate war upon a State, is meant that the authorities of the United States cannot be maintained or the laws enforced, if a State organization interpose to annul them, or protect its citizens in doing so, nothing could be more erroneous. The Constitution unquestionably contemplated this very contingency of adverse State interposition or legislation, and provided against it and for the *National supremacy*, in the clear and imperative language which has already been quoted. *This supremacy may be maintained by the whole physical power of the nation, and whoever offends against the law is subject to its penalty, in whatever official robes or insignia he may be clothed.*

The supremacy of the laws of this country have been maintained by the prowess of Americans, and the people of this country have satisfied themselves that they have a Government. The question which will now cause some discussion is the re-organization of States which have been in rebellion against the Government. But they are not the only States—*all* having been regenerated require reconstruction. *Special* privileges by legislation and *Slavery*, the first an arrogated, and the second a ceded private wrong, which were interfering with the rights of States, now lie prostrate in the cold embrace of death, and their dead bodies remain to be expelled from our legislative and judicial tribunals where they disgrace American law.

We have yet to deplore a faction in our midst, who are mean and dishonest enough to advocate the repudiation of the National debt, another word for rebellion. "Like causes," philosophers assure us, "produce like effects;" you will therefore be prepared to meet the repudiator of the public debt, as you have met the advocate of secession; you will indignantly repel the unfounded suggestion. It is a violation of the eternal principle of law, and I believe it is not commendable for any man in this country to counsel in direct violation of the imperative language of the Constitution, "That *private property* shall not be taken for public use without just compensation." This question is easily settled under the first general *maxim* of interpretation—that it is not allowable to interpret what has no need of interpretation.—(*Vattel, Book II., Ch. XVII., Sec. 26.*)

Degraded and fallen must be that man, who, in his sober moments, could advise the American people—a people rich in resources, possessed of a high sense of National honor, the only free people on earth, and this, too, in the face of an observing world—to impair the obligation of a contract by taking private property for public use without just compensation; and in many instances from honest, hard-working people; while on the other hand, they allow a questionable class of men who have obtained millions through fraud and deceit, and thus, to say the least, have technically aided rebellion, to enjoy, uninterrupted, their ill-gotten gain. For instance, men contract with the Government to furnish its defenders (the soldiers) with good and wholesome provisions for a stipulated sum— but heedless and unmindful of the sacred covenants in contracts— influenced by that sordid principle in man denominated as "the root of all evil," they violate the truth in that contract by furnishing inferior provisions, and thereby weaken the defence of the Government by rendering the soldier less able to endure the fatigue of battle, thus aiding and assisting the enemy; and this is not all, the Government is robbed of a large amount of money which has to be paid by the people. Now, instead of advocating the repudiation of the Public Debt, in which individuals are equally bound to pay out of the property acquired under the protection of its laws, as they are to defend it against internal assaults and external enemies with their lives, both of which was made manifest during the administration of Abraham Lincoln, it appears to me there would be more logic, if not sense, in thus advocating the confiscation of the property of all men who have taken the advantage of this vile attempt to assassinate our Political Life, to rob and plunder the Government. Aside from the Constitution, this Government cannot repudiate the public debt under the rule of common law. "The master is responsible for the act of the servant." The people, who, by the way, constitute the Federal Government, are responsible for the acts of all the servants in their employ, and those servants personally responsible to the people, who by the principles of this Government constitute their master. In the language of Andrew Johnson, the time has arrived when the American people should understand this fact.

When we come to consider the ridiculous controversy which men have entered into on the subject of repudiation, and seriously reflect that all their arguments have tended to show a total want of common-place knowledge, we ought to hide ourselves from the derision with which foreigners must look upon our credulity. Among those who have been thus employing themselves, I must not forget to notice Jeff. Davis, who was one of the first to start the scheme, when he endorsed the repudiation of the State debt of Mississippi. From that moment his career has been an onward one of infamy, until at last he repudiated his manhood, and took refuge under a petticoat, to be dragged thence before the tribunals of his country to be tried for the crimes and treason he had been guilty. Davis is a fair specimen of that proud class who scoffed at Abraham Lincoln as unfit for his station. Not the rich and proud, but the poor and lowly, will be the favorites of an enfranchised Republic. The words of the prophet will be fulfilled: "And I will punish the people for their evil, and the wicked for their iniquity, and will lay low the haughtiness of the terrible. I will make a man more pre-

cious than fine gold ; even a man than the golden wedge of Ophir."
I catch these sublime words of prophecy, and echo them back as
the assurance of triumph :

Oh, why should the spirit of mortal be proud ?
Like a swift, fleeting meteor, a fast-flying cloud,
A flash of the lightning, a break of the wave,
He passeth from life to his rest in the grave.

The leaves of the oak and the willow shall fade,
Be scattered around and together be laid ;
And the young and the old, and the low and the high,
Shall moulder to dust and together shall lie.

The infant and mother attended and loved ;
The mother and infant's affection who proved ;
The husband that mother and infant who blessed,
Each, all, are away to their dwellings of rest.

The hand of the king that the sceptre hath borne ;
The brow of the priest that the mitre hath worn ;
The eye of the sage and the heart of the brave,
Are hidden and lost in the depths of the grave.

The peasant, whose lot was to sow and to reap ;
The herdsman, who climbed with his goats up the steep ;
The beggar, who wandered in search of his bread,
Have faded away like the grass that we tread.

So the multitude goes, like the flower or the weed,
That withers away to let others succeed ;
So the multitude comes, even those we behold,
To repeat every tale that has often been told.

For we are the same that our fathers have been ;
We see the same sights our fathers have seen ;
We drink the same stream and view the same sun,
And run the same course our fathers have run.

The thoughts we are thinking our fathers would think ;
From the death we are shrinking our fathers would shrink ;
To the life we are clinging they also would cling ;
But it speeds for us all, like a bird on the wing.

They loved, but the story we cannot unfold ;
They scorned, but the heart of the haughty is cold ;
They grieved, but no wail from their slumber will come ;
They joyed, but the tongue of their gladness is dumb.

They died, aye! they died ; we things that are now,
That walk on the turf that lies over their brow
And make in their dwellings a transient abode,
Meet the things that they met on their pilgrimage road.

Yea! hope and despondency, pleasure and pain,
We mingle together in sunshine and rain ;
And the smile and the tear, the song and the dirge,
Still follow each other, like surge upon surge.

'Tis the wink of an eye, 'tis the draught of a breath,
From the blossom of health to the paleness of death,
From the gilded saloon to the bier and the shroud,
Oh, why should the spirit of mortal be proud ?

Fellow-citizens, your task is before you—mourn not the dead,
but rejoice in his life and example. Rejoice as you point to this
child of the people who was lifted so high that Republican institutions became manifest in him. Rejoice that through him emancipation of those two worms that were gnawing at the vitals of the
Republic—those two private wrongs that were encroaching on
public rights—Slavery and Special Privileges was proclaimed.
Above all, see to it that his constant vows are fulfilled, and that the
promises of our fathers are maintained ; see that you maintain invi-
olate that contract signed by them with a pen of diamond dipped
in that sacred fountain of Principle in which they sought *Security*
and *Justice*. Pride, falsehood and deceit had no point within their
breast from which its radii could diverge. That towering monster,
Falsehood, should never pollute American tongues. All writers on
constitutional and statutory construction agree that the meaning
of the framers is the Constitution and the Statute. What then did
the framers of the Constitution mean by the following language :
" Congress shall make no laws abridging the freedom of speech or
of the press ?" Did they mean to give you an unlimited permission
to slander the Government and its officers at your pleasure and take
refuge behind the letter (which is but the shadow of the spirit), and
plead the above language in bar ? Remember that the common
law was adopted by the framers of the Constitution as the law of
our land, barred only by statute, which is well known to all
lawyers. And we are informed by the Hon. Ogden Edwards
that the common law was conceded by the people of England to be
the grand charter of liberty. And this very able jurist, in his lec-
ture on Legal Science, declared, " that the Common Law was, as it
were, the title deed by which men held their rights, and that the
faults and errors arising under the common law are more frequently
from the ignorance of judges and the prejudice of jurors than from
the common law itself." And its author, Sir William Blackstone,
informs us that the common law was dictated by God himself,
therefore binding over all the globe. The immortal Cicero long

since observed : " In every thing the consent of all nations is to be accounted the *Law* of *Nature*, and to resist it is to resist the voice of God." And, believe me, the Common Law is as much the Title Deed by which the Federal Government holds its rights as that of an individual, and was no doubt intended by the framers of our glorious Constitution as the legal remedy against the abuse of truth, which our fathers intended to be freely spoken, printed and discussed on all public matters. On the contrary, in private matters, the citizen is held in restraint from the fact that malice is inferred of which the law does not and cannot take cognizance.. Is this question, then, completely settled in the negative ? Certainly it is settled to the satisfaction of all who pin their faith to mere human authority. But human authority seldom settled any thing with me ; for whatever I have had an interest in knowing the truth, I have generally appealed from the decree of that unsatisfactory court to the less fallible decision of the court of fact. And what does fact say in this instance ? *Fact* says, that the Constitution is a piece of God Almighty's law, sought not in precedent but in principle by those venerable fathers in their united appeal to Nature —for to Nature—eternal Nature must Truth ever make her first and last appeal. But how do I know all this, you will ask—I who hold modern legislation in horror ! I will tell you truly—I first guessed it ; for I could not suppose that Government, unlike every other great *revolution* of *matter* could be either less than *attraction* which brings things or their atoms into closer proximity, or place them by the force of *repulsion* at a greater distance from each other. Still not being a person easily satisfied with guess-work, I took the trouble in this particular instance to interrogate Nature. And as sure as the sun ever shone on this earth, Nature completely verified the fact of my anticipation, that *attraction* and *repulsion* are the two grand forces by which, not the motions of this Government only, but the motions of the Universe are kept in control. They are the two powers or forces, *male* and *female*, which not only produce motion everywhere and in every thing, but are endowed with the Divine power of creating and forming every thing in nature—the solar systems and their mineral, vegetable and animal kingdoms. What is *ambition* and *worldly disgust*, but a modification or effect of *attractive* and *repulsive* influence. For example : ambition, by its *attractive* influence, brings things or their atoms into closer proximity. On the contrary, worldly disgust, by its *repulsive* influence, places them at a greater distance from each other. Therefore, let babblers beware how they commit themselves in this matter ; let them fully understand, that when they deny the duality of motion in all things, or that the Constitution in the *abstract* is deficient, they not only arraign God for His goodness, but expose at the same time their utter ignorance of His laws. Where men have not examined, surely it were only policy to be silent.

But I anticipate a question which has been put to *Moses*, to *Socrates*, to *Gallileo*, to *Columbus*, to every man that has presented the face of *Independence*, and which , green-eyed Envy never yet has failed to accompany with the sneer of detraction : " *Who are you, that you dare to presume to know more than we ?*" Free from that cowardly, bastard modesty, which trembles to own its competency before the scorn of malevolence, I frankly answer as a freeman, that I set out with the *cardinal principle* that *might* and *right* belong, equally and exclusively, to the People ; that in them resides all sovereignty ; that there is no power on earth which may rightly subject them to any laws or restraints, of body or mind, which they choose not to adopt for themselves; that government is for their own comfort and protection, and not for the special benefit of the governors ; that *magistrates* are *servants* and officeholders' *agents* whom the People create and at pleasure control or remove. That they are intrusted with temporary duties for the execution of which they are responsible to the People as their masters, and the People responsible for the act of their servants.

This subject is one of great interest, of which it behooves the American people to be fully informed, but which it is to be feared is more frequently spoken of than understood. The mass of our citizens are so much engaged in their private affairs that this great matter is in no considerable degree neglected.

Suffer not yourselves to be cheated by an echo, or led by party for party purposes. Do not be deceived by the pretense of morbid sympathizers with secession, that because the Southern Confederacy has been forced to surrender, our Government ought to abandon her ground. That ground was taken to resist two great and crying grievances, the attempt to strangle the infant breath of the Declaration, " That *all men* are born *free* and *equal*," and the special privileges, and extensive combinations of selfish interests enforced under a protecting statute. Fellow-countrymen, arouse from your lethargic slumber, and proclaim in a voice like many thunders, the spirit of tyranny cannot exhibit itself in this country by monopolizing legislation or title or rank. Orders of nobility, primogenitive rights, inherited rank and birth-right privileges of every kind, have been exterminated by the bravery and wisdom of our patriotic ancestors. Americans are brethren, and among brethren there exists no invidious distinction. By the principles of this Government a king is reminded that though a crown adorns his head and a sceptre his hand, yet the blood in his veins is derived from the common parent of mankind, and is no better than that of the humble individual. It acknowledges Christ as the only Potentate, King of kings, and Lord of lords. Then hail, thou glorious *principle* of Liberty, bright transcript of all that is amiable ! Hail, thou blest in political science which so beautifully exemplifies the Church of Christ ! Welcome ye delightful mansions where all enjoy *peace, tranquillity* and *liberty* to worship the great Giver of all good gifts and graces according to the dictates of their conscience, to conform to His will, and to conduct themselves as under the ALL-SEEING EYE ! Welcome ye blessed retreats where the poor and oppressed flee for security, and where is dispensed freedom and equality to those unfortunate exiles from their homes and their friends, with unbounded liberality! Welcome sacred habitations, where privileged gentlemen never dwell, where all men politically meet on a level! I say unto you, lift up your heads, ye sons and daughters of Columbia! The Lord of hosts is with you, whose arm is not shortened. The Lamb is upon Mount Zion with his hundred-forty-and-four-thousands, gathering his numberless host from the four winds. Cast off all unrighteous and selfish interests. Let not the love of this world's goods weigh you down. Stand upon the watch-tower; put on the whole armor of God; give no place to the Devil; quench all the fiery darts of the wicked within; then will ye not fear what man, or the sons of men, can do unto you! The God of Jacob is your refuge, who will break the bow of the ungodly, and snap the spears asunder, and burn their chariots in the fire, and make desolation in the earth. He is fulfilling the promises of old made to His chosen, who will give nations for them, and people for their life. I say, ye sons and daughters of the land of equal rights and equality, stand faithful, and be valiant for Liberty and Truth upon the earth. For it is against it they are fighting within and without, that it might fall and be extinguished from the earth, and that equity and righteousness may not enter the nations who have said in their hearts, "Come, let us kill the heir, and the inheritance will be ours." But in vain do the heathen rage, and the people imagine such foolish things. For their hope shall perish and their purpose be made void; they shall never bring to pass the thoughts of their hearts, the Lord hath spoken it; for the seed of evil doers, shall never be renowned. Wherefore, if ye hear of wars, or rumors, or commotions, or pestilence, or famines, or the rushing of the ungodly, like the noise of the raging sea which cannot rest, let not your hearts be troubled, the Lord of heaven and earth, who is above all, will rebuke the devourer for your sakes; for your redemption draweth nigh, when ye see these things come to pass.

So, fear God, and prize your precious privileges of equal rights. This is what I desire you all should enjoy, and you never can enjoy this in its fullness unless you maintain the principles and follow the examples of that long list of patriots and sages that signed the Declaration of Independence, and of those who framed the great charter of our liberties.

CHAPTER II. ˙

I SHALL commence the subject of Reconstruction of the Union in the language of Andrew Johnson, President of the United States. In him we have a man of similar origin with Mr. Lincoln; equally a child of the people, equally in sympathy with their reasoning, and, perhaps, better informed as to the true condition and governmental necessities of the Southern States. Self-educated, and exalted by perseverance through years of laborious industry and sacrifice, no accident of a moment can be accepted by the judgment of our people as reversing Mr. Johnson's claim to the confidence and respect of the country. And I have yet to find the first man who has any thing to say thus far against his Administration. I have not seen either Whig or Democrat, or any other stripe of politician in the country, since he assumed the reins of Government, who has aught to complain of. Therefore it is difficult for me to meet or combat any objection to the Administration of President Johnson. One notable thing has fallen under my observation since he assumed the reins of power, and that is his proclamation in regard to the reconstruction of the Union. But I have not heard any opposition to that; indeed, my friends, the principles upon which the proclamation was founded are the principles that were announced by Mr. Lincoln. It is not necessary for me to advance any argument here, but it strikes me that when the people nominated Andrew Johnson and Abraham Lincoln, it was on the avowed principle, that has been announced over and over again, that when the people of the Southern States laid down their arms they should again be received into the Union. Rebels have the power to forfeit their own personal rights, civil and political; but they have no power, directly or indirectly, to work the destruction of a State, it being only bequeathed in trust to the people. We are only trustees, charged with sacred rights; ours to use, ours to enjoy, but not ours to subvert; possession in the people, but the title in our fathers, who received them from the Eternal Father.

President Johnson informs us " that the time has arrived when the American people should understand what *crime is*, and that it should be *punished*, and its *penalties enforced* and *inflicted*. Who is there here who would say that the assassin who has stricken from our midst one beloved and revered by all should not suffer the penalties of his crimes? Then if you take the life of one individual for the murder of another, and believe that his property should be confiscated, what should be done with him or them who have attempted the life of a nation composed of thirty millions of people? Yes, treason against a State, treason against all the States, treason against the Government of the United States, is the highest crime that can be committed, and those engaged in it should suffer all its penalties. Treason must be made odious; treason *must be punished and impoverished*. They must not only be punished, but their social power must be destroyed. If not, they will still maintain an ascendency, and may again become numerous and powerful; for in the words of a former Senator of the United States, "When traitors become numerous enough treason becomes respectable." And I say, that *after making treason odious, every Union man and the Government should be remunerated out of the pocket of those who have inflicted this great suffering upon the country*. But do not understand me as saying this in a spirit of anger, for, if I understand my own heart, the reverse is the case. And while I say this, as to the lead-ers' punishment, I also say leniency, conciliation and amnesty to the thousands whom they have misled and deceived. Some are satisfied with the idea that States are to be lost in territorial and other divisions—are to lose their character as States. But their life-breath has been only suspended, and it is a high constitutional obligation we have to secure each of these States in the possession and enjoyment of a Republican form of government. *A State may be in the Government with a peculiar institution, and by the operation of rebellion lose that feature.* But it was a State when it went into rebellion, and when it comes out without the institution, it is still a State. *I hold it as a solemn obligation in any one of these States where the rebel armies have been beaten back or expelled—I care not how small the number of Union men, if enough to man the Ship of State—I hold it, I say, a high duty to protect and secure to them a Republican form of Government.* This is no new opinion. It is expressed in conformity with my understanding of the genius and theory of our Government. Then, in adjusting and putting the Government on its legs again, I think the progress of this work should pass into the hands of its friends. If a State is to be nursed until it gets strength, it must be nursed by its friends, not smothered by its enemies. Now, permit me to remark, that, while I have opposed dissolution and disintegration on the one hand, on the other, I am equally opposed to consolidation, or the centralization of power in the hands of a few." These are President Johnson's words, and these are my views. The reconstruction I meditate, unlike many extremists, is at least free from the imputation of disorganizing the States in rebellion; on the contrary, I would restore all their citizens who have not forfeited their rights, by their own voluntary act, to their original nationality. The voters, in whose hands now lies the power of the ballot, should take warning of other nations; they should consider the ways of God in his creation of the Universe, and remember that he made every thing to give comfort and delight, and minister to the wants of *all;* and that he did not intend the few should control and sport with the many for the furtherance of their own private and selfish ends.

On the 13th of April (a day for ever to be held in inauspicious remembrance, like the *dies Aliensis,* in the annals of Rome), the citizens of Charleston claimed it as their special privilege to make a target of the standard of United America, the pledge of her Union and the symbol of her power, which so many gallant hearts had poured out their life-blood on the ocean and the land to uphold. Then, for the first time, a State portrayed the appalling fact that political demagogues had, up to that hour, been, to a man, in all but utter darkness, treading the paths of special privileges, which leads to misery's most gloomy abodes. Was it, then, wonderful that an event so startling should fall upon the American people like a thunderbolt. This aroused all Americans from their lethargic slumber, and stimulated them to cry, in a voice like many thunders, Down with the power of this traditional ceded monster Slavery and consign him irrevocably to the shades of oblivion. These resolutions were immediately disseminated through the North and West; the tongue and pens of high-minded patriots and well-informed men labored incessantly in the holy cause; the fire of liberty, like a volcanic eruption, blazed forth from the press and burst forth with indignation from the head and hearts of Young America; the flames spread far and wide, and, like volcanic lava, it seemed to scorch and wither every thing that interposed to impede its onward progress, overthrowing that ceded monster Slavery in its march and casting him into the shades of oblivion.

Yes, let oblivion be the dungeon for this voracious spoiler of equal rights, and let a timely, considerate and firm resolution be his jailer, and reason and philanthropy be the chains that bind him in his cell in such a manner as to render escape impracticable; then, and not till then, can American freemen boast of equal rights in *law* and in *fact.*

But in order to accomplish this glorious work of incarceration, it may be necessary that we take a retrospective view of a few by-gone years to enable us to call to mind scenes sufficiently dreadful to make us stand aghast, and view with awe and astonishment the crimes which are inseparably connected with the baneful practice of privileging gentlemen by Legislature; and this, too, by a people who have no legal right to give one man or set of men special privileges that others do not enjoy; and it follows that our servants who are sent to represent their masters in the legislative halls have no authority to exceed the rights of the people unto whom they are personally responsible. This eternal principle of equal rights, being derived from God, is supreme, and will, if rightly applied, neutralize the *virus* of arrogated power now lurking behind the shield of special statute, and stimulate the people to substitute in lieu thereof public statutes of limitation authorizing the formation of corporations, and thus open the avenues which leads to the fundamental spring of free and unalloyed liberty, from which issues a strong and limpid stream, bearing on its bosom that righteous and American principle of equal rights—the bounteous gift of Nature's God—to that small host of infant freemen who, at the risk of all that was dear to man, secured by deed and conveyed them in trust to their political heirs and assigns for ever. These sacred covenants Abraham Lincoln maintained and presented to the wicked disciples of a false but unwavering monopoly, as the beacon of the triumph of enduring faith over the agonizing pangs of oppression. As yet I have only assailed the principle of that system of arrogated power which is incorporated under the sanction and bound together by special statute, carefully avoiding individual attack. If it be said I have used language too strong for the occasion, I answer in the words of Burke: "When ignorance and corruption have usurped the *professor's chair*, and placed themselves in the seats of science and virtue, it is high time to speak out. We know that the doctrines of folly are of great use to the professors of vice. We know that it is one of the signs of a corrupt and degenerated age, and one of the means of insuring its further corruption and degeneracy, to give lenient epithets to corruption and crime."

Lord Bacon informs us, that if disciples only knew their own strength they would soon find out the weakness of their masters. What led him to this conclusion? What but the fact, that, with all his ability, even he (Lord Bacon) had been duped by his teachers? And why did Des Cartes say that no man could possibly pretend to the name of philosopher who had not, at least, once in his life, doubted all that he had been previously taught? He, too, had been hoodwinked by his pretended masters in philosophy. But *you*, perhaps, will say that all these took place in olden times; the world is quite changed since then; professors, political and civil, are now the most enlightened and respectable men alive; they go to church, where they are examples of piety; they never were found out in a lie; are not subject to the passions of other men; have no motives of interest or ambition; in fact, they are all but angels. Now, I only wish you knew the manner in which the most of these very respectable persons (Jeff. Davis, for example) get their offices; the tricks, the party-work, the subserviency, meanness and hypocrisy practiced by them for that and other ends, and you would not so tamely submit your judgment to their theoretic dreams and delusions. Methinks if men were but seriously and conscientiously to *observe* the preponderating influence which rank, wealth and power have bestowed upon the upper classes of society, and how prone they are, at all times, to sacrifice their own judgments at the shrine of high-sounding titles, and *compare* them by the scale by which all things ascend to unity, on *reflection*, they would almost despise themselves, and detest a system of real, but unobserved, and as such, unheeded slavery. It matters not what constitutes the master, if a man is in bondage he is a slave! A mere glance at the passing events of the day, will, to a steady observer, convince us that we have all retrograded in every thing like manly and honorable feeling; that we have become *idolators* of the worst character, and rendered ourselves subservient to the will and wishes of tyrannical monopolies and imbecile politicians. The parties of our day boastingly exult in the chimeras of delusive schemes; they compound theories they do not understand, and insist that a slavish people, like modern Americans, should obey, humbly obey, a mass of folly garnished by a worse than a superstitious dread of disobeying caucus nominations concocted by knaves and countenanced by fools!

The greatest politician, the most sublime orator, the most eloquent writer, the mightiest reasoner, the most heroic Christian of Adam's race, has said, "In the mouth of *two* or *three* witnesses shall every word be established." Yet there is a class of scornful sceptics, skillful in fighting with shadows, but not observant of the substance, who call themselves politicians, orators, eloquent writers, reasoners and Christians, who will not believe the testimony of a hundred witnesses that the regeneration of American law by Abraham Lincoln has removed precedent and re-established the principle of our fathers in the fullness of their declaration, and restored the Constitution under the first maxims of interpretation; that he has regenerated American law, from the black and sombre shades of falsehood, to be reconstructed upon the everlasting and eternal principle of truth, and that his blood cries forth from the ground.

In the appropriate language of Kossuth: "Gentlemen of the Bar, you have the noble task to be the first *interpreters* of the law; to make it subservient to *justice*, to maintain its *Eternal Principles* against the encroachments of *facts;* and to restore those principles to life, whenever obliterated by misunderstanding or by violence, when darkness is cast upon the light of truth. It is one of your noblest duties to apply principle to show that an unjust custom is a corrupt practice, an abuse! It was this eternal principle that pervades all Nature—the moving power of creation—that Abraham Lincoln maintained against the encroachment of rebellion; and to this eternal principle—the common law of *all* matter—every change in the Government is subjected. That the power by which the national motions are influenced is the same that influences the motions of every kind of matter. Therefore you must by this time be convinced that the principle of American law is only declaratory of, and acts in subordination to, that all predominant law of God's eternal motion. For example, we read in the Gospel according to John, that "In the beginning was the word, and the word was with God, and the word was God." Now, it was the *security* of all men in equal and exact *justice*, settled by the eternal word of truth, that our fathers sought to build the fortress of our liberties. Justice and truth, united in one, form the eternal principle of the American Government. It was through the eternal motion of the word of God that our fathers declared *all* men to be free and equal; and it was through the same eternal motion that Abraham Lincoln had his being; it was through the same eternal motion that he applied those hallowed words of our fathers, in the full finition of their truth, in equal justice to *all*. It was the violation of this eternal word of truth in contracts and affirmations that caused our wayward brothers to rebel. The violation of truth in contracts and affirmations and promises, has involved nations in destruction, undermined the foundation of public prosperity, blasted the good name and the comfort of families, perplexed and agitated the minds of thousands and millions, and thrown contempt on the revelation of Heaven and the discoveries of science.

If, according to Lord Bacon, "disciples do owe unto masters only a temporary relief, and a suspension of their own judgment *until they be fully instructed*, and not an absolute resignation or perpetual captivity," you will not be sorry to escape from the thraldom of men who, when asked for bread, gave you a substance which, in the darkness of your ignorance, you could not by any possibility tell was a stone! No longer mocked by mystic gibberish, you will now take your places as judges of the law you formerly, implicitly, and without examination believed; and according to the arguments which I have placed before you, you will pronounce between *precedent* and *principle*—whether the division of American law into Federal and municipal is founded in Nature and reason, or whether, in the words of the same great philosopher, "all things do by scale ascend to unity."

The written Charter of our National Liberties guards against a dynasty of hereditary rank or of legitimate descent. It has not, however, proved a safeguard against the dynasty of modern States, "that of associated wealth." It appears, then, that one channel remains for the spirit of aristocracy to pour its entire flood. Here facts encroach upon the eternal principles of law; and here it becomes our bounden duty to maintain the *eternal principles* of *law*, which escaped extermination by the bravery and wisdom of our patriotic ancestors.

One weak point exists in the fortress of our freedom—it is that which may be assailed by the *engine* of combined wealth. One order of nobility is not guarded against; an order unentitled, it is true, but possessing attributes more radically injurious to popular rights than all the empty insignia of foreign aristocracy; it is based not upon the respect which is naturally paid to the descendants from a long line of illustrious ancestors, but upon the influence of that sordid principle in men, which the greatest of all reformers in religion and politics characterizes as "the root of all evil." Wealth is the grand engine of self-exaltation and of popular oppression in this country. Such is the nature of our institutions, that the love of domination, inherent in the human heart, has here no other outlet. Of all inventions which have been put in operation in this country to promote the inordinate accumulation of wealth, the most exceptionable are *incorporated companies*. The very object of an incorporated charter is to give its possessor artificial powers and special privileges not enjoyed by others, or an exemption from the liabilities to which others are subjected. It may reasonably be doubted whether the whole system, from beginning to end, is not an infraction of the

Constitution. It is at least an evasion of its plain provisions, pernicious in its influence upon industry and morals, and meriting the firm resistance of all true lovers of equal rights.

Under the dark and sombre shades of this custom, and pursuing the dubious paths of precedent, our youth grow up to man's estate with borrowed notions of political science from foreign governments, and thus lose ·sight of the cardinal principle that all power belongs to the people. It is difficult for men, whose minds are thus formed, to feel that the undue superiority of wealth and rank they may chance to obtain, must devolve a corresponding privation upon other men who, by the laws of Nature and the principles of our Government, are equally with themselves entitled to the enjoyment of these privileges. These are hard lessons for men to learn who are born to the possession of superior social and intellectual enjoyments, and who forget that the nature of our institutions forbid them engrossing privileged superiority. In a government like ours, where all power and sovereignty rests with the people, the exercise of this right and the consequent expression of public interest and public feeling is, on ordinary occasions, a matter of deep concern, but at a period like the present, of vital importance. Pause, vain man, and behold the ocean of misery and river of blood which had their origin in the unjust evasion of the plain provisions of the Constitution. Pause, I say, while you tread the spacious halls of those gorgeous mansions reared by the receipts of special privileges by the few who seek protection under the strong arm of arrogated power of the Legislature, with act on act, till the cope-stone intersect the floating clouds. Woe unto them, for by them have offenses come.

We should look with a jealous eye upon the usurpation of power in legislation, such as conferring public rights on individuals. It is an old saying that laws were never made for honest men : this would imply that all persons, encircled by any protecting statute, must be dishonest and a parcel of rogues : hence the protection offered to those monopolists, the modern Shylocks of the nineteenth century. These men not being honest, are compelled to seek shelter under the strong arm of a disgraceful enactment, and veil their own stupidity under the garb of arrogated power, rendered mischievous and dangerous by law ! Under existing circumstances it becomes the imperative duty of the American Government to protect its weaker citizens from the encroachments of individuals, and more especially from the jointure of two or more, and withdraw all countenance from a system calculated only to neutralize the Declaration of the Fathers, to say nothing of the daily recurring scenes of poor and helpless females struggling for support, perchance for some infirm and helpless relative against wealth and power in the hands of avaricious and soulless men, which everywhere meet our eyes ; and to extend its protection to the Declaration of our Fathers, by elevating it to that rank in public estimation to which its importance and merits so well entitle, it, that each one of its atoms

3

may apply principle to show that the unjust custom of special
statute to promote private interests is a corrupt practice and an
abuse of the Cardinal Principle of Democracy.

To illustrate this, I need only to refer you to the railroad monopolies which surround you on every side. Those monopolists, by their
schemes, which are more fully developed every day, have now wound
themselves up to such a pitch as cannot but rest the reins of Government and cause mankind to sing the heart-pungent chorus of the
prophetic tablet on the Mosaic harp of *ten strings* (*the ten command-
ments*), "How is the gold become dim! how is the fine gold
changed!!" Truly, these monopolies are an awful picture of human
depravity! they are the slaveholders of the North. Individual
rights their slaves, and their *special charter*, the lash by which they
coerce the free-born American into submission to their arrogant and
overbearing rule. Not satisfied with the usurpation of municipal
rights, these ambitious monopolists and heartless usurpers of the
rights of men have carried their avaricious and delusive schemes
into the Federal Legislature, in order that they might receive impetus from the gigantic motive-power of the nation, and, sorrowful
to relate, have succeeded in extending their peculating propensities,
under the special privileges of the Federal Legislature—infringing
not only on individual rights, but also upon the rights of the me-
tropolitan State of New York. Remember, that a State bears the
same relation to the Federal Government as an individual does to
the State. This serves as a glass for all to behold the encroachment of the Federal Legislature upon the rights of the State of New
York. That a citizen of a town is a citizen of a county, a citizen of
a State, and a citizen of the United States has, by our recent strug-
gle, been placed beyond dispute. Therefore, the Federal Government has an undoubted right to pass laws imposing a tax upon its
citizens and regulations for collecting the same; but when it assumes
the appointing power of the collectors, it most assuredly exceeds
its authority. Here, then, we have an infringement on the sacred
rights of *all* the citizens of the State of New York, and upon the
individual slave who is lashed into obedience to the peculating man-
date of special privilege.

With the most childish simplicity some submit to the extreme
tyranny of arrogated power. Instead of using the *eyes* that God
has given them, they shut them in the most determined manner,
that their *ears* may be the more surely abused. Silly, simple
Brother Jonathan! Why will you pin your faith to fallible and
fallacious authority, when you may get the truth so easily by a
little personal examination? To be able to discriminate in the
choice of a servant, and to guard against political imposition, would
not cost you half the time nor any thing like the trouble of master-
ing the inflection of Vebero, or *Amo amare!* Which kind of knowledge is of most use in life, I leave to pedants and philosophers to
settle, meantime I shall beg your attention while I refer back to
first principles, for I believe it is a truth that those who do not refer

back to first principles will go to decay. What was the first principles of our fathers in the formation of this Government? It was *equal* and *exact justice* to *all*, quickened into *life* by the illuminating *light* of the eternal Word of Truth. What was the first principles of the Lord's people in an early day? It was the principle of light and life; an unerring principle that would always guide in the path of safety, and which will enable you, as it has me, "to restore the eternal principles of law to life, whenever obliterated by misunderstanding or by violence; whenever darkness is cast upon the light of truth. But how can you brush away the cobwebs of ages from the windows of truth, without rousing the reptiles and insects that so long rejoiced in the darkness these cobwebs afforded—the bats and spiders, to whom daylight is death? *Truth*, like a torch, does two things; not only does it open up to mankind a path to escape from the thorns and briers which surround them, but, breaking upon a long night of ignorance, it betrays to the eye of the newly awakened sleeper the bandits and brigands who have been taking advantage of its darkness to rob and plunder him. What has truth to expect from these? What but to be whispered away by the breath of calumny; to be scouted and lied down by the knaves and fools whom interest or intercourse has leagued with the public robber as his partizans! "To abandon usurped power," says Robertson, in his History of Scotland, " to renounce lucrative error, are sacrifices which the virtue of individuals has, on some occasions, offered to truth; but from any society of men no such effort can be expected. The corruption of society, recommended by common utility and justified by universal practice, are viewed by its members without shame or horror; and reformation never proceeds from themselves, but is always forced upon them by some foreign hand."

Facts and experience convince us that Andrew Johnson was right when he said that the time had arrived when the American people should understand what crime was. Yes, fellow-citizens, facts and experience convince us that it is time the reign of falsehood should cease; it has ruled the world with an iron grasp; thousands have been the victims sacrificed at its shrine. Let revolution, revolution in ideas, be the cry through mountain, glen, valley and plain, until this hydra of falsehood, combination and arrogated privilege be shorn of its fangs. Truth is mighty and must prevail, and commends itself to the human mind. Custom, interest and ignorance growl brutally or scoff foolishly; but growls and scoffs cannot subdue Truth, nor drive it out of the field; it is destined to pursue the last of Error's whelps to a deeper den than that to which Putman drove the Pomfret wolf; and if it come forth again to light, it must come as Putman brought forth his—dragged out dead to feast the eyes of righteous execration. Thanks be to the untiring wing of wisdom, which has kept up the march during the reign of Abraham Lincoln's Administration, this thick and sombre cloud of arrogated power, conferred on a privileged few, has been virtually cast into the shades of oblivion, and there, together with its ceded kinsman, slavery, chained for ever (as I hope in God) by an indignant and outraged people.

> " The day has broke, and God's just stroke
> On hypocrites must come ;
> Their many words and carnal swords
> Can't save them from their doom."

I will now, if patience will permit, give you a test by which you may know the difference between error and truth, the pettifogger or perverter of truth, and the shyster who sneaks around its eternal principle—a test that cannot possibly deceive you—the result of that inductive process which has elicited the cause of universal motion.

We read in the London *Times* of March 7, in a leader, " That the Government at Washington announces that this very summer will see Federal unity not only restored but ready for Federal action. They make no secret of their intention to present an enormous list of damages, which they are quite aware we shall not acknowledge. Their own public writers admit that the law, as settled by the chief American authorities, is against them, and that the precedents of American practice is against them ; but they hold that the unexampled magnitude of the occasion removes the question out of law and precedent, and justifies the Americans in making new precedents instead of following old ones." This unexampled magnitude of the occasion should convince the world of mankind of the impropriety of standing still on the line of precedent while all around is in motion ; matter being ever in motion, contributes to the magnitude of this unexampled occasion. Therefore, it would seem as if the most superficial observer could perceive that Americans have nothing to do with precedent, they being a motive people. But listen one moment to an American statesman, who not long since, stated in the Assembly of the United States, " that the slave trade, as well as slaves, was a very ancient practice, and that in former times, and in almost all parts of the world, it was carried on." It is ancient, no doubt. But there is another more ancient practice, not altogether unconnected with slave trading—I mean the practice of murder, and of the worst sort of murder, fratricidal murder ; for it does so happen that the first man that was born murdered the second, and that second-born was his brother. But I do not think you would deem it a palliation of the offense of murder or of fratricide to cite its undeniable antiquity.

When I, for one, reflect on the crime of depriving a man of his own free will in United America—in a Government founded on *equal justice to all*—I am constrained to acknowledge that this crime was ceded upon the colonies by Great Britain, and that after the Revolution it was through sufferance, under pecuniary difficulties, left to individuals to regulate by the State laws. There is one species of crime, however, upon which I must be permitted to say a word—I mean the schemes of avaricious monopolists, incorporated by legislation into laws, to enable them to charge whatever their avarice may demand. From the present system of acquiring property, we may trace the loose disregard of duty in legislative halls, a corrupt administration of law in judicial functionaries, and a higher estimate set upon cunning and device than upon skill and integrity; things incompatible with the stability of a Republic and destructive to the rights of man.

Our *security* and the equal and exact justice to all, is founded on the principle of eternal truth, by those inspired fathers to whom God was pleased to give the American decalogue—the Constitution—which declares that no one shall be deprived of life, liberty, or property without due process of law. That no Legislature shall pass an *ex post facto* law, or law impairing the obligation of a contract. This Constitution has established a Government with the highest attributes of sovereignty, thus rendering the authority of the United States, within its sphere, supreme. This is a *vital principle*. It was so regarded by the framers of the Constitution, and they have secured it in the most explicit and emphatic terms. " This Constitution, and the laws made pursuant thereto, shall be the supreme law of the land, and the judges in every State shall be bound thereby, any thing in the constitution or laws of any State to the contrary notwithstanding." This vital principle of the Federal Constitution is the great controller of every court, and the true key to all good practice, reflecting a light in the midst of our judicial departments more brilliant than the diamonds on a monarch's crown, and will, if understood aright, render more safe and easy the passage through the intricate windings of the mazy labyrinths of American law, limiting the duties of the courts to the defining of law, and the rendering of equal and exact justice to *all.*

And, further, to secure the rights in man derived from God, our fathers covenanted to and with each other that private rights shall not be taken for public use without just compensation, and entailed this imperative obligation by deed of trust on their heirs and assigns for ever, thereby making it imperative on the Legislatures to fully secure each individual in his rights, and in no single instance to lend their aid in the encroachment of a private right on the public rights, or *vica versa.* These covenants of our fathers reflect a mutual lustre on each other, and, like the radii of a circle, they all diverge to the same point, and lead directly from the liberty of the individual man and individual State up to the unity in the liberty of *all* these United States.

Was there ever such a field in which to plant the seed of an immortal harvest? So vast a ship, so richly laden with the world's treasures and riches, whose helm is offered to the guiding influence of every forming institution, with equal and *exact justice*, security on one side and the principle of eternal truth on the other; and these, blended in one, form the eternal principle of American law. The true meaning of the word Principle is Unity. The practice of law, therefore, consists in maintaining this *eternal principle* against the encroachment of *facts*. In order to illustrate this subject, I shall offer a few brief remarks on ancient usage. Not long since a case was decided by the Supreme Court of New York against the plaintiff, on the ground that it was not usual to allow grace on checks. This was a case where the check was dated ahead, and made payable at one of the banks in the city of New York, and protested by said bank on the day of maturity for nonpayment. Subsequently, and within the limitation of three days, the maker called to take the check, and was informed that there was an additional charge for protest, to which he demurred; and hence the suit to recover damages for the encroachment of the fact of protest upon the eternal principle of law. Not feeling disposed to submit to the decision of the Supreme Court of the State, he appealed to the Court having appellate jurisdiction, where he maintained the security of his rights, in justice with the principles of truth, against the encroachment of that protest, and was sustained by the Court of Appeals.

A contracts with B to build a house, A placing his own construction upon the words in the contract, and guided by the sordid principle of gain, misunderstands their righteous meaning, and thus violates the sacred truth in contracts to his pecuniary advantage. Here the eternal principle of law is obliterated by misunderstanding. And here B applies the security of his rights in justice to the principles of truth, and thus remedies the breach in the contract, and restores the principle of law to life. When the truth, in the above contract, is willfully violated, then it is that the eternal principle of law is obliterated, and is to be restored to life as above. To accomplish this, and to relieve us from the undue weight of false pretense (false representations of all denominations), our late lamented President has handed to us the *lever* and *fulcrum*. Let us, then, make use of our instruments. This instrument was not manufactured by special statute, but by the eternal principle of American law, under the motive influence of legal construction, in subordination to that all-pervading principle commented upon by Blackstone and appreciated and applied by Vattel, Book II., Chap. xvii., secs. 263 and 282.

Vattel informs us that, by the first maxim of interpretation, it is not allowable to interpret what has no need of interpretation. An attempt, therefore, to interpret a principle of law, written in plain English, would be an attempt to pervert the principle of law and the meaning of the writer, and constitutes what is commonly called pettifogging and shystering around an *eternal principle*, casting darkness upon the *light* of truth. Here, then, it becomes our bounden duty to apply the *security* of our *rights* in *justice* with the principle of eternal truth. One bright ray from this great luminary of union would send a world of such fog into the ocean of oblivion.

Blackstone informs us that "all human laws are only declaratory of, and acts in subordination to the divine law." Such being the fact, it must appear evident to every impartial reasoner, to every unprejudiced son and daughter of Columbia, from the humblest laborer to the most renowned statesman, theologian and man of science throughout the length and breadth of the land, from the regions of the Aroostook to the banks of the Rio Grande, from the shores of the rock-ribbed Atlantic to California's golden sands, that, as God is no respecter of persons, it is an absolute violation and direct disobedience of the divine law to tax the title of property in a poor man to its full value under the heavy pressure of mortgage, and that mortgage taxed by government as the personal property of the rich man. It is no palliation of oppression to know that the private property of the poor man is exempt from tax—it is not equal and exact justice, for all are not situated alike : instance the farmer and the merchant. Here we should apply principle to show that this unjust custom is a corrupt practice and abuse.

But, says one, the lawyer informs us that custom makes law in the absence of all written law. So it does, so long as that custom is within the limits of the eternal principle of American law. Remember matter is ever in motion and ever changing ; but this principle is eternal and unchangable. This is the reason Kossuth declared it one of the noblest duties of the lawyer to apply principle to show that an unjust custom is a corrupt practice and abuse.

According to Blackstone, the revealed law is of greater validity than the moral law ; therefore, you have only to turn to the pages of Holy Writ and you have before you the law in all things pertaining to government and rules for the regulation of society. The disposal of riches, the *necessity* for *labor*, the folly of *idleness*, the evil of abominations of every grade, the fruits of intemperance in all things, the punishment of unholy lusts, the sin of him who taketh away the bread of the poor, and of him who enslaveth the people in political bondage—upon these, and upon all things wherein the mind of man has ever run, does this great book of God speak the language of inspiration in the words of soberness and truth, and which, if they were but observed, would lead to the interpretation of our Constitution in harmony with the security, justice and truth our fathers breathed into it at its first *birth*. As the spring flows from the fountain and partakes of its qualities, and as the shadow always accompanies the substance, and is produced by it, so the liberty of the individual man uniformly accompanies the security of the rights of all in the full majesty of equal and exact justice, with the principles of eternal truth blended in unity, and is produced by the powerful influence which this governing principle exerts over the mind. Thus, you see, we are governed by a law which pervades the whole moral universe wherever it extends, which can never be rescinded, and which, like the law of gravitation in the material world, connects all the individuals of which it is composed in one harmonious system ; one great principle binds them together ; God, in his unity, pervades them all.

We anticipate, from the administration of Andrew Johnson, an immediate passage of the gulph which separates the present from what is to come, and bars the way from the world of to-day to the brighter world of the future. *Onward* is the law which destiny has impressed upon the American people and the American Government. Gravitation is not more inevitably the quality of matter than progress is the lot of the democracy of the United States for all time to come. In the arts of peace, our position is transcendent; on the land we have built already the tallest and most substantial monuments; and the almost undivided mastery of the seas belong to the genius and principles which upholds so proudly, and waft in the winds of heaven so nobly, the surmounting flag, blazing all over with the Stars and Stripes, those consecrated emblems which marshal the way of peace, liberty and self-government for the whole family of nations. The issue, during President Johnson's administration, is not only a question of great domestic measures, but also is the issue of our external relations, and the assertion of our rights to the highest place in the family of nations, and the ascendency of republicanism in every quarter of the globe; if need be, ultimately and gradually, but rather at the earliest convenient opportunity. It is only thus that our internal tranquillity can be preserved. Ourselves must teach, and our children must learn, that quiet at home can best be preserved by mixing with strangers, talking about the world, and taking a general interest in human affairs.

Let us cast our eyes over the earth and observe the great dual divisions of the human race—the East and the West. One half of the old world continues without improvement, and without ideas, beneath the weight of a barbarian civilization. Contrast with a European or American family an Eastern one; the former is based upon equality, the latter upon polygamy and slavery, which leave to love its brutal fury, but which deprives it of its sweet sympathy and divine illusions. " For love is of God."—1 John iv. 7. Education gives at once grace and government to genius. Without it, what is *man?* A splendid slave, a reasoning savage, vascillating between the dignity of an intelligence derived from God, and the degradation of passions participated with brutes! Americans, be Americans; think for yourselves, free as Republicans ever should think; consider the price of your liberties, and stand more upon your independence and less on the line of precedent, while all around you is in motion. To illustrate this, I need only refer you to every steamer which ploughs its way to and from our shores, every new vessel which spreads its sails to the ocean winds, every mile of railway which is constructed, every new line of telegraph which is established—those iron nerves along which thrills the electricity of thought—all the physical and mental advances which characterize this age above others, contribute to bring in contact and close dependence, not only individuals and communities, but nations themselves. To-day the capital of France is nearer to

Washington than it was twenty years ago; and the Message, which then required weeks in the tardy transmission from one portion of the Union to another, now outstrips the sun and annihilates time. The printing press, steam and the telegraph, have utterly changed the relation of men and things; and the policy which, under previous conditions, was wise and true, would now be false and foolish. Remember there is but one principle and many natures in matter, and that matter being ever in motion contributes to this change. Men, communities and nations under the new order of things must react upon each other with new force, and, however imperceptibly, influence each others fortunes. To adhere to old traditions, and endeavor to shape our course by the old charts of precedent, under these altered circumstances, can only be the counsel of Rheum-eyed senility, which cannot and should not control the conduct of this generation. And those who quarrel with the spirit of the age, and the general tendencies of events, impugne the wisdom of heaven, and set up their weak intellects against that divinity which, in the fullness of time, gradually and surely works out its beneficent designs.

Fellow-citizens, trust not to parchment! trust not to precedent! for, as I have already told you, the history of the world is filled with precedents of tyranny and oppression; and parchment regulations deceived the people of Virginia. No man had more experience in the government of that State than its political father, Mr. Jefferson; no one had more fearlessly pointed out the defects of their Constitution. Unfortunately it imposes no check upon the legislative power; their Governor is elected by the legislature, and of course is but a creature of that body. Mr. Jefferson, in his Notes on Virginia, expresses himself thus : " All the powers of government, legislative, executive and judiciary, result to the legislative body. The concentrating these in the same hands is precisely the definition of despotic government. It will be no alleviation that these powers will be exercised by a plurality of hands, and not by a single one. One hundred and seventy-three despots would surely be as oppressive as one. Let those who doubt it turn their eyes on the Republic of Venice. Little will it avail us that they are chosen by ourselves. An *elective despotism* was not the government we fought for; but one which should not only be founded on *free principles*, but in which the powers of government should be so divided and balanced among several bodies of magistracy, as that no one could transcend their legal limits without being effectually checked and restrained by the others. For this reason, that convention which passed the ordinance of government, laid its foundation on this basis, that the legislative, executive and judiciary departments should be separate and distinct, so that no person should exercise the powers of more than one of them at the same time." Here, then, we have the opinion and the complaint of this great man. The legislature of Virginia had usurped the power of all the departments. The people had declared that those departments should be independent, but they deceived themselves by trusting to parchment regulations.

Distinct branches are not only necessary to the existence of government, but when you have prescribed them, it is necessary that you should make them, in a great degree, independent of each other. No government can be so formed as to make them entirely separate; but it has been the study of the wisest and best men to invent a plan by which they might be rendered as independent of each other as the nature of government would admit. The legislative department is by far the strongest, and is constantly inclined to encroach upon the weaker branches of government, and upon individual rights. This arises from a variety of causes. In the first place, the powers of that department are more extensive and undefinable than those of any other, which gives its members an exalted idea of their superiority. They are the representatives of the people, from which circumstance they think they possess, and of right ought to possess, all the powers of the people. This is natural, and it is easy to imagine the consequences that may follow.

In reconstruction of the Union, it appears to be our duty, almost to fix anew, the principles of representation for a free people. The first question for our consideration is, whether it is wise and proper that a restriction of any kind should be placed upon the legislative power? On that subject it would seem that little doubt can remain. That a check of some kind is necessary has received the sanction and been confirmed by the experience of ages. A large majority of the States in the Union, in which, if the science of Government be not better understood, its first principles are certainly more faithfully regarded than in any other country, have provided restrictions of this sort. In the Constitution of the freest Governments of Europe, the same provisions are adopted. That a restriction is proper we are all agreed; and the question arises, is the amendment that I am about to propose more desirable and better adapted to perform the office intended than the present system of representation? To arrive at a just conclusion on this subject it will be necessary carefully to consider the design of such a check and the advantages which are expected to result from it. Its object is, first, to guard against hasty and improvident legislation, to protect all departments from legislative encroachment; but more especial to protect public and private rights against legislative encroachment, and to protect labor against capital. With regard to the first of these objects—the protection against hasty and improvident legislation—the system of every free Government proceeds on the assumption that checks for that purpose are wise, salutary and proper. Hence the division of all legislative bodies into distinct branches, each with an absolute negative upon the other. The talent, wisdom and patriotism of the representatives could be thrown into one branch, and the public money saved by the procedure; still experience demonstrates that such a plan tends alike to the destruction of, public liberty and private rights. They adopted it in Pennsylvania,

and it is said to have received the appropriation of the illustrious
Franklin, but they found that one branch only led to pernicious effects. The system endured but for a season; and the necessity of
different branches of their Government to act as mutual checks upon
each other was perceived, and the conviction was followed by an
alteration of their Constitution. The first step, then, towards check-
ing the wild career of legislation is the organization of two
branches of the legislature. Composed of different materials, they
mutually watch over the proceedings of each other. And having
the benefit of seperate discussions, their measures receive a more
thorough examination which uniformly leads to more favorable
results. But these branches as now constructed are kindred bodies
and it might sometimes happen that the same feelings and passions
would prevail—feelings and passions which might lead to dangerous results. This rendered it necessary to establish a third branch,
to revise the proceedings of the two; but as this revisory power
has generally been placed in a small body or a single hand, it is not
vested with an absolute, but nearly with a qualified negative. And
our experience has proved that this third provision against hasty
and unadvised acts of the legislature has been salutary and profit-
able. The people of this State have been in the habit of looking at
the proceedings of the legislature thus constituted, and they have
been accustomed to this revisory power. Their objections have
never been that this revisory power existed, or that it was distinct
from the legislature; but they do complain that it is placed in improper hands; in the hands of persons not directly responsible to
the people, and whose duty forbids all connection with the legislature. I am one of those who fully believe in the force and effici-
ency of that objection.

That Legislative Bodies are subject to passions, and sometimes
to improper influence, is not to be denied. Mr. Jefferson com-
plained, in 1781, of the Constitution of Virginia, because the two
branches of the Legislature were not sufficiently dissimilar, but he
did not point out the mode in which he thought that object could
be best effected. That matter was reserved for further explanation,
and another set of circumstances. That time is born, and the day
has dawned upon this gigantic young republic. Methinks I hear a
voice emanating from an oppressed but mighty people, like the low
moanings of a distant but heavy clap of thunder to arouse them to
put the *veto*, from which there is no appeal, upon the unhallowed
doings of the whole race of monopolists. Let them either rank
under our *Dual Banner*, and grant the subsidy of their countenance
to our warfare; or, should they espouse the same philanthropic
cause, we shall content us to volunteer under theirs, and become
their humble pioneer in beleaguering the hitherto redoubted bul-
warks of our mutual foe! It must come to this: and I rejoice
already to observe many symptons of coalition that will ultimately
crown the principle I advocate with triumph. This dual system of
regulating the motion of legislative representation must be esta-

blished. Such is the gravitating tendency of society that no spont
taneous effort at arms-length will hold it up. It is by the constan-
energy and strong attraction of our powerful institutions, now
complete with the *cope stone* placed upon them by Abraham
Lincoln, only that the needed intellectual and moral power can be
applied : and the present is the age of forming them. If this work
be done, and well done, our country is safe, and the world's hope
is secure. The government of force will cease, and that of intelligence and virtue will take its place ; and nation after nation,
cheered by our example, will follow in our footsteps till the whole
earth is free.

I would but vilely fulfill the trust which I have imposed upon
myself, did I, in accordance with the fawning hypocrisy of the day,
flatter and mislead the public, from whose liberality I have reaped
so much, and from whom I hope to deserve a further continuance.
I take it, therefore, for granted, that *plain honest truth*, ungarnished
by metaphysical research, will best suit the tastes of honest men.
With these sentiments, under the divine influence of the Eternal
Motion of the Word of God, I will now place before you, for your
consideration, a new *representative system*, founded upon the two
grand forces by which not the motions of government only,
but the motions of the Universe are kept in control ; and by these
forces, and no other, can political life be influenced, either for good
or for evil, whatever be the nature of the natural agent by which
they may be called into play.

It is a matter of some surprise to me that Duality of Motion has
not more generally engaged the attention of the Professors of
legal science. Indeed, by this dualty of *movement,* and no other—
attraction and repulsion—I am compelled to explain every variety of
change which our Government assumes, for throughout all creation,
we find unity the effect of diversity or repetition. There can be no
symmetry without this; the most rugged line you can portray.
when opposed to its perfect repetition, immediately becomes a
design, a unity. Man in the abstract, is a unity of the two sexes
The unity of the individual man is made up of a duplex repetition
that pervades his entire configuration outwardly as inwardly. The
life of man in all its functions is a thing of periodic repetitions.
His passions in like manner are duplex, joy, woe, confidence, fear,
love, hate, are examples. All things, then, have two aspects. The
UNITY of action of RICH and POOR is proved by the duality of
Motion and Improvement, which *capital* and *labor* is capable of
producing.

The unexampled magnitude of the occasion justifies the reconstruction of our legislative system, and the establishing of a more
effectual dual check-and-balance system to regulate the motion of
American Legislation. For example, let the *rich* form *one,* and the
poor the other, house of the Legislation. Then, and not till then,
will capital and labor be equally represented. Then will this great
popular government of self-rule rest upon those three substantial

pillars, Wisdom, Strength and Beauty. Wisdom to contrive, Strength to sustain, and Beauty to adorn. Individual to contrive, Capital to sustain, and Labor to beautify and adorn the material furnished by capital, and execute the plans laid down on the great trestle board by the people, upon the demonstrated truths of mathematical science. Guided by those eternal and unchangeable truths which this science unfolds and demonstrates, the illustrious Isaac Newton determined the properties and the composition of light, the cause of the alternate movements of the ocean, the mechanism of the planetary system, and expanded our views of the grandeur of the Universe and the perfection of the Almighty Contriver. Need you, then, be told, that these principles are applicable to legislation throughout every part of the universe, and must be recognised by all intelligent Legislators? Therefore, not presuming to dictate, but humbly suggest that each member of our Legislatures be individually reformed to that famed dictate, which the Oracle of Delphos pronounced to Cicero, "Follow Nature!" —not in the confined sense of our mortal economy, but in every department of her works. One great principle bind them together —God in his Unity pervades them all! That God, who fills all immensity of space, and is everywhere present. He is in everything that he has created : why, because nothing that he has created can subsist without his power ; therefore, every *effect* must rest upon its *cause*. He is in every plant, in every tree, and every animated creature ; but in a special manner he manifests his power in the hearts of his rational children, because he has made them governors of this lower creation, and has fitted them to govern it. Now, as we submit to his power, and wait for his Light and Life in the soul, all the other creatures remain with us a blessing, and all unite in praise to him, even the least animal on earth. And yet see what a state and condition men have fallen into. They even oppress their own fellow-creatures and take his rights from him— they destroy his free agency, which the Almighty never did. Here they usurp a power above God Almighty, and bring their fellow-creature under bondage by man's power. They take away that in which all blessing consists ; for, without the exercise of this free agency it were better that he had never been born. The whole is a departure from the guidance and influence of the Holy Ghost; for all who have kept under this, as the blessed Jesus recommended them to, have been led unto all Truth and out of all evil, and they have walked safely and gloriously under his government, he being their King and Captain.

Now this doctrine or principle of government that people talk so much about, if they understood as they ought, would lead to no contention ; and it would seem that the most superficial observer could perceive that Americans have nothing to do with precedents. Our Fathers sought security and justice not in precedent but in *principle*, and the war from which this country is just emerging should teach the world of mankind that America makes rather than follows Precedent. Principle, then, and not Precedent, should be the guiding star of the American people. The application of this Eternal Principle of Law to matter, is fully delineated by Kossuth, in his address to the members of the New York bar. I yield to him, as his just due, the origin of the reformed application of this principle of law to matter, and to Abraham Lincoln, as the martyr in the supreme moment of its permanent crowning. I take credit to myself, however, for being one of the first to carry it into effect.

The evil, perhaps I should say fallacy, of following precedents of nations governed by minorities, naturally led me to ask, Can this be the proper practice? It was assuredly the practice of others—of all. Could all be wrong? Reflection taught me that men seldom act for themselves, but take, for the most part, a tons or bias from some individual master.

By education most have been misled :
So they believe because they were so bred.

Fellow countrymen, I have had the resolution to think for myself —aye, and to act; and my conviction, gained from much and extensive experience, is, that all questions of National Law rest upon the eternal principle or moving power of matter. But let it not for a moment be supposed, that in thus sweepingly arraigning the present system of legal policy, that of applying precedent instead of principle, I have the remotest wish to degrade the profession of the law. It has ever, on the contrary, been my object to improve the social position of that noble order. Nor do I presume to dictate, but in order to render it useful, honorable and honored, I would most humbly suggest that the observations of one of the boldest and most eloquent of American writers, Dr. Channing, of Boston, be observed and appreciated by every member of the profession. "Intellectual culture," says this justly eminent person, "consists, not chiefly, as many are apt to think, in accumulating information, though this is important; but in building up a force of thought which may be turned at will on any subject on which we are forced to pass judgment. This force is manifested in the concentration of the attention; in accurate penetrating observation; in diving beneath the effect to the cause; in detecting the more *subtle* differences and resemblances of things; in reading the future in the present; and especially in rising from *particular facts* to general laws or universal truths. This last exertion of the intellect, its rising to broad views and great principles, constitute what is called a philosophical mind, and is especially worthy of culture. What it means, your own observations must have taught you. You must have taken note of two classes of men; the one always employed on details, on particular facts, and the other using these facts as foundations of higher, wider truths. The latter are philosophers. For example, men had for ages seen pieces of wood, stones, metals, falling to the ground. Newton seized on these particular facts, and rose to the idea that all matter tends, or is *attracted* towards all matter, and then defined the law according to which this attraction or force acts at different distances; thus giving us a *grand Principle*, which we have reason to think extends to, and *controls* the whole outward CREATION. One man reads a history, and can tell you all its events, and there *stops*. Another *combines these events*, brings them under ONE VIEW, and learns the great causes which are at work on this or another nation, and what are its great tendencies, whether to freedom or despotism, to one or other *form* of civilization. So one man talks continually about the particular actions of this or that neighbor, while another looks beyond the acts to the inward principle from which they spring, and gathers from them larger views of human nature. In a word, one man sees all things *apart* and in *fragments*, while another strives to discover the harmony, connexion, UNITY of ALL."

That such unity, fellow-citizens, does actually and visibly pervade the whole subject of legal science, harmonizing with the history of every other thing in nature, the experience of twenty years' practice in medicine has fully convinced me. One great principle binds them together ; God, in his UNITY, pervades them all !

It was a beautiful speculation of Parmenio," remarked Lord Bacon, "though but a *speculation* in him, that all things do by scale ascend to unity." Do I need to tell you that every thing on this earth which can be weighed and measured is MATTER—matter in one form or another, and that there is but one principle, one eternal principle, that pervades all matter ! What is the difference, then, between the practice of law and the practice of medicine ? A mere difference of degree. The former practices in the *first*, and the latter in the *second* degree. The same eternal principle is applied by both. Who in his senses, then, would deny that the lawyer is bound by the conjunction *and*, in his oath of office, to blend in UNITY the municipal and federal laws in one body and apply to the subject-matter ? If the wants of the entire body of the people are studied, as the physician studies the wants of every part of the human system, instead of one or two parts only, and leaving the rest to sicken and decay, the permanency of the nation will be rendered more certain, and stability receive greater guarantee. This serves as a glass for the American people to behold the unity of law. The word *law*, when applied to individuals or nations, is an abstract term, expressive of the *sum total* of harmonious movements, produced by the *principal forces* in nature, when acting together with perfect periodicity in one body, and applied by the lawyer to restore an individual or national right, whenever impaired by misunderstanding or by violence, or when darkness is cast upon the light of truth. But, sorrowful to relate, the writers on American law, pursuing a false mode of analysis, have, for a long time, been engaged in dividing and subdividing the subject, until it reaches its acme in the elaborate and ponderous terms of the learned and classical professors, who have long been engaged in splitting straws, blowing bubbles, and giving a mighty great degree of weight to feathers.   Of which, such is the extent of subdivision and subtility attained by these authors, that the lawyers are plunged into oceans of vapor and often lost in the fog.   Thus, mystified by theory, man, presumptuous man! has dared to divide what God, as a part of creation, united; to separate and pervert what the Eternal, in the wisdom of his Omnipresence, made entire!

Creation being a UNITY on which all laws depend, it follows that no change or disorder of government can be explained without having recourse to the sciences, which are the laws of the universe. Here we find the thread of the analogy, by which we can reason from induction and proceed from demonstration.   This mode of reasoning has enabled me to give you a system of American law, established upon the immutable laws of the terrestrial and planetary motions, derived from magnetic phenomena with their attendant influence on political life, as the result of that inductive process which has elicited the cause of Universal Motion.

We read in the Scriptures of the Everlasting Gospel, that "In the beginning God created the heavens and the earth.   And the earth was without form and void; and darkness *was* upon the face of the waters.   And God said let there be light, and there was light."   Motion, heat and temperatural changes.   *Light* produces motion, *motion* produces heat, and *heat* produces changes of temperature.   There can be no *motion* in *matter* without change of temperature, and no *change* of *temperature* without motion in matter. This is so indisputable an axiom, that Bacon and others supposed motion and change of temperature to be one and the same.

The *motive power* of a republic must be greater and more rapid than that of a despotism, inasmuch as all such movements can only result from the action of *intellect* on *matter*.   Where that action is greatest, there physical and material progress, wealth and strength, and means of effective action in war or peace, must be proportionably great.   Both our individual and Democratic enterprise have thus brought conquest to the very threshold of the ancient dame who relies on her aristocratic birth and 'her liveries.   And while a noble steamer of our own construction, the Baltic, of the Collins' Liverpool line, which has shown that, in steam as in sails, American enterprise can beat any thing not American, has distanced the most recent British construction, and now steams her way into the harbor of New York the victor of the old order; she checks her wheels, blows a powerfully loud whistle of astonishment, sends up three cheers, and lets off innumerably brass crackers, as the Gabriel annunciatior of a new and more salutary birth, moves along in the face of wind and tide.   A new era has been opened to the world, by genius, in the caloric ship Ericsson; a new element has been conquered to the use of man, and the abundant air of heaven has been chained to the beam and crank, and it soon will be to the car and the factory.   Henceforth, as the "snail carries his house upon his head," so all men will find their great motor, imponderous and ubiquitous, in the air about them. Gentle aerials, which transport you to infinite distances, float in every breeze, and people, by science, the circumambient air with magic creatures hitherto invisible save to fancy. Poetry becomes tangible and calculable by vulgar aerometess; and the lover's sigh may no longer waft a kiss to his mistress, but be deposited in a warming cylinder, and so carry along to her steadily himself. Thus every advance leads to another, and the triumphs of Democracy are not raised in columns of skulls, but are fashioned by the arkwright and the smith; are not formed in desolution, but in the creative power of science. Therefore, O, man! come to thy centre, like all other creatures and forms do. Ye men of learning and science crowned, come to the centre of science— the triune *Chemistry, Magnetism* and *Electricity* around which the sciences revolve and gravitate. Surely no man, professing to be in the least conversant with the physical sciences, would now dispute, what Mr. Faraday was the first to prove, that all *three* are, in reality, mere modifications of one great power.

The more you reflect on this subject, the more you must come to the opinion, that all things, at last, are only modes or differences of one matter. Their approach to unity may be traced through every thing in *nature*. Betwixt the history of the human race, for example, the revolutions of empires, and the history of the individual man, the strongest relations of affinity may be traced. The corporeal revolutions of the body, like the revolutions of a kingdom, are a *series* of *events;* time, space and motion are equally elements of both. "An analyst or a historian," says Hume, "who would undertake to write the history of Europe during any century, would be influenced by the connection of TIME and PLACE. All *events,* which happen in that *portion* of space and *period* of time are comprehended in his design, though, in other respects, different and unconnected. They have still a species of UNITY amid all their DIVERSITY."

That the material atoms of government do follow the laws to which all matter is subject, under the particular circumstances in which the matter composing them is placed, Sir William Blackstone, the author of Common Law, bears unequivocal testimony. He says that, "When the Supreme Being formed the universe, and created matter out of nothing, he imposed certain principles upon that matter from which it can never depart, and without which it would cease to be. When he put that matter into motion he established *certain laws* of motion to which all moveable bodies must conform.

"The *law* of motion being coeval with mankind, and dictated by God himself, is, of course, *superior in obligation to any other. It is binding over all the globe, in all countries, and at all times.* No HUMAN LAWS ARE OF ANY VALIDITY if contrary to this; and such of them as are VALID derive all their force and all their authority, mediately or immediately from this original. Human laws are only

4

declaratory of, and act in subordination to, the Divine law. Instance the case of murder. This is expressly forbidden by the Divine, and demonstrable by the natural ; and from these prohibitions arise the unlawfulness of this crime. Those human laws that annex a punishment to it *do not increase* the *moral guilt* or superadd any *fresh obligation, in foro conscientiæ*, to *abstain* from its perpetration. Nay, if any *human law shall allow or enjoin us to commit it, we are bound to transgress that human law*, or else we must offend both natural and Divine law."— *Vide* Blackstone's Commentaries, 1 Chit., pp. 25, 27, 28.

This is what I wish to impress upon American legislators, who represent a great and mighty people, and who themselves are atoms of this gigantic young republic. Let this ETERNAL PRINCIPLE, then, be your motto and your mark, and do not forget the practical application. Remember that the LIGHT of NATURE and the dictates of REVELATION both conspire to demonstrate the eternal destiny of *united liberty*. Permit me here to say to the enemies of united constitution liberty, if their hatred cannot be appeased, they may prepare to have their eyeballs seared, as they behold the steady flight of the American eagle on his burnished wings, for years and years to come.

Let us here, in these United States, where individual rights are understood, and where man's more noble and better nature, and the faculties which raise him above the brute, are allowed and encouraged in their widest scope and freest exercise, where the life of intellect flows full and strong through every individual, and animates every member of the political body, erect a high *tower*, composed of Religious, Political, and Domestic Freedom, and *totally* abstain from all combinations, *ecclesiastical, political* or *civil*, and build thereon a beacon which shall shed its rays over our Legislatures, so that, through the medium of its light they may be guided through the dark mazes of anti-American combinations, and follow in the wake of that great Light that lighteth every man that cometh into the world ; which ever has, and ever will, direct, with an unerring index, to the scale by which all things ascend to Unity.

It is the bounden duty of American Legislators to follow the leadings and the counsel of God ; for he leads his people and guides their feet in the paths of *Wisdom ;* and he alone is the saving *health* of all nations ; and without Him they can do nothing that is good and acceptable in his sight. Let their eyes be towards Him, who is invisible, dwelling in the Light ; and neither act or speak out of his fear and counsel ; then will they be preserved to his praise, and to their eternal comfort and peace, And whatever they do, let all be done in *faith* to the glory of God ; for what is not in *faith* is sin. So shall they be kept steadfast on the *Immovable Rock*, legislating laws parallel with the streams from the Fountain of Nature. This may serve as a glass for all lawyers and judges to behold the fallacy of precedents, and the Legislature as merely a candlestick, bearing the Light of the Eternal Principle of American Law, and enable them to follow the Light instead of the stick—that Light which emanates from the great First Cause.

This Eternal Principle applied by the *Lawyer*, *Doctor*, and *Minister*, in harmony with the scale by which all things ascend to Unity, has become one of the most useful, if not one of the proudest works of the human intellect. And let no one approach it with inutility or imbecility. This Eternal Principle, or *male* and *female* forces, are innate in every kind of matter, without possessing any character in common with it, whether it be ponderable or imponderable ; and in their organized or magnetized state, they were the foundation of the solar system, and of the mineral, vegetable and animal kingdoms. *Repulsions, Expansions, Attractions, Contractions, Systematic Action, Motion,* and *Form,* are then in this order, the Attributes of these Forces, by which that system and these kingdoms were formed, with a precision, and adorned with a beauty, that defy imitation. Nothing can therefore equal the adaptation of these forces to produce such results, for besides their unlimited power, which can make a world tremble like a leaf, the great velocity of their motions and their almost inconceivable tenuity, enable them to penetrate the most minute orifices, and construct an infinite variety of bodies of every form and size, and produce motion in the smallest structure with the same geometrical accuracy as in the largest.

This eternal principle when applied by the lawyer, doctor or minister to the subject matter, is an abstract term expression of the *sum total* of harmonious movement produced by the principal forces in Nature when acting together with perfect periodicity in one body. It is the same eternal principle that passes up the tender plant, causing it to mature and fructify ; and the same *principle,* when it lies dormant in the seed till the season arrives when the same all-pervading principle, floating and basking in the sun-beams, whispers to the seed, " arise from the dead !"

All Nature is subservient and obedient to this all-potent voice. And the high intelligence of man, and his lofty reason, owe all their force and superior excellence to this most refined and God-like principle. As well might it be said that there are *three, six* or more Gods, as to say that there are *three* or *six* different principles. No philosopher has ever said so, and no philosopher can say so. Here, indeed,

> "A little learning is a dangerous thing ;
> Drink deep, or taste not this Pierian spring.
> Here shallow draughts intoxicate the brain :
> But drinking deep sobers it again."

Every day you hear people talk of a " principle" of a thing, but really without knowing what they are talking about : the true meaning of the word " principle" is unity—something simple or single, to which we may specially refer in the midst of an apparently conflicting variety. That a perfect unity pervades all the Federal and municipal laws is indisputable, and of the correctness of a unity or principle to guide American lawyers and legislators there is as little doubt.

The demonstrated principle of science is eternal and unchangeable and is applicable to the *municipal Government* of the several *States* as that of the general Government or other movable matter. And the flights of the loftiest genius that ever appeared on earth, when compared with the rapid movements of this principle, the *motive power* of creation may be no more than as the flutterings of a microsopic insect to the sublime flights of the soaring eagle. If any one should condemn this method of demonstration because it is plain and inartificial, I would have such a one know that only weak people dispise things for their being simple and plain; and that I am ready to serve the public, though I lose my reputation by it. And I will say, that I do not at all question were it not for common prejudice that the said *unity* of the municipal and Federal law might be *accommodated to the subject matter in adjudication in all our courts*, and thus silence forever their conflicting decisions. The beauty, the harmony, the symmetry of this unity, nobody but such as prefer books of Precedents to the Book of Nature and Common Sense would be so ignorant as to question.

Under the Divine influence of principle, we shall see the truth triumph, the temple of idols overthrown and the seat of falsehood brought to silence; for we are in the presence of the All-Seeing Eye, that God who is just and merciful. I hope we all believe this, and if so, we must feel that He cannot by any means justify injustice in the least degree; for there is nothing but justice that can recommend us in the Divine sight. And justice is the great paladium of our security in the bonds of eternal truth—this unity is the foundation of American Independence. It was upon this unity or principle that Abraham Lincoln founded a Nationality on Democratic Principles, which was one of his greatest works, and one which marked the first great epoch in his history. The *Emancipation* Proclamation was the central *act* of his administration and the central *fact* of the nineteenth century. And it was this same principle—the eternal motion of the Word of God through an earthen vessel—when, in 1861, Daniel S. Dickinson said, "I stand upon the Constitutional ground of my fathers. Then I will stand and animate my countrymen to stand with me, and when once we *shall* have peace restored—when we *shall have* put down rebellion, when we *shall have* encouraged fidelity, when peace and prosperity *shall* again greet us, then let us see if any *individual is wronged, if any are deprived of their rights.* See that equal and exact justice is extended to all." These are his words and this is my case. We must be merciful as well as just; we must possess this most excellent virtue, charity; and we never can have that virtue till we are just, because justice is the foundation of every virtue. Virtue is true nobility, and wisdom the channel by which it is directed. Wisdom seeks the secret shade, the lonely cell designed for contemplation; there enthroned, she sits delivering her sacred oracles; there let us seek her aid in applying principle to show that the unjust custom of legislative grants to individuals at the public expense is a corrupt practice and an abuse of the cardinal principle of Democracy. It is certainly believed that our legislative halls have, in repeated instances, been made the theatres of the most exceptionable and unprincipled political bargains and coalitions, in which men acted, not from the honest dictates of their consciences and with a single eye to the public interests, but from the unworthy motive of personal aggrandizement, not only disconnected with the public good, but in many instances to direct hostility against it. It is equally true, that in proportion as these charges have been credited abroad, the character of our state has sunk in the estimation of all honest men, and the eternal principle of law obliterated by violence and darkness cast upon the light of truth. It is not my intention at this time to enter into the truth of these charges. But inasmuch as the *military engineer* has completed his work, it becomes the bounden duty of the *civil engineer* to take the helm of public state and probe them, as well as other transactions of a deeper cast, and still more injurious in their effects upon our public character, to their inmost recesses; to separate the innocent from the guilty; to vindicate the great body of our citizens from the charge of participating in the profligacy of the few, and to give rest to that purturbed spirit which now haunts the scenes of former moral and political debaucheries, to the end that this great and otherwise flourishing nation, no longer be retarded in her march upward and onward to what I feel and know God intended it should—the centre of freedom for the whole earth, and the place where he will delight to manifest His presence.

In conclusion, I will take my leave of you in the language of our martyred President: " With malice towards none, with charity for all, with firmness in the right, let us strive on to finish the work we are in, to bind up the nation's wound, to care for him who shall have borne the battle, and for his widow and for his orphan; to do all which may achieve and cherish a just and lasting peace among ourselves and with all nations." His words are ended; his voice is hushed in death. This is his last legacy. His lips are closed and he shall speak no more. But there is a voice that speaketh even now. I have heard that voice from heaven say to me, that the principles he maintained against the encroachment of that black and sombre cloud of rebellion, shall be conveyed by the eternal motion of the Word of God through earthen vessels till the second coming of Christ and the kingdoms of this world become his kingdom.

.

www.ingramcontent.com/pod-product-compliance
Lightning Source LLC
Chambersburg PA
CBHW021642270326
41931CB00008B/1134